Dandelion

Memoir of

a Free Spirit

Dandelion

Catherine James

ST. MARTIN'S PRESS ❧ NEW YORK

The names and/or identifying characteristics of several people have been changed.

www.stmartins.com

Design by Kathryn Parise

Photograph by Mike Zellers

LIBRARY OF CONGRESS CATALOGING-IN-PUBLICATION DATA

James, Catherine, 1950–
    Dandelion / Catherine James.—1st ed.
        p. cm.
        ISBN-13: 978-0-312-36781-7
        ISBN-10: 0-312-36781-3
1. Parent and child—Memoir.   2. United States—History—1969—
Memoir.   3. Counterculture—Memoir.   I. Title.
PS3610.A4285D36 2007
813'.6—dc22   2007020318

First Edition: October 2007

10 9 8 7 6 5 4 3 2 1

For Mimi

Acknowledgments

To Damian, for being my wonderful son and grounding force.

To Pamela Des Barres, who insisted and believed I could do it on my own.

To Patti D'Arbanville, who patiently listened, read, and reread my manuscript.

To Roger Daltrey, who has always stood by me and urged me to write.

To Dennis Weiler, for being the most supportive person on the planet, and for teaching me how to use the computer.

To Ovid Pope, who always took the time to help me with my endeavors.

To Gabriel Byrne, for all the inspiring books.

To my agent, Peter McGuigan, who made it all possible.

To my editor, Elizabeth Beier, for her gentle guidance and encouraging enthusiasm.

To all the extraordinary people who have graced my life. Thank you.

Dandelion

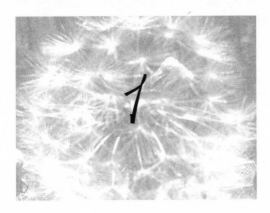

*T*he first time I saw my father as a woman was at the grand old restaurant Musso & Frank Grill on Hollywood Boulevard. He had called me the week before asking if we could meet for lunch, as he had something important he wanted to discuss. It sounded serious, but he didn't want to speak about it on the telephone. I had my suspicions as to what the conversation might be about, but nothing could have prepared me for that notable afternoon.

I arrived at noon, and Musso's was buzzing with its regular upscale crowd and a battalion of aging Italian waiters who were as stiff as the white table linens.

My heart sank when I saw a frightful-looking character coyly flagging a paisley handkerchief in my direction. I thought, "Dear God, please don't let this be my father."

The distant sight of him made me feel faint, like I was being pulled to my knees by a magnetic force. I'd grown up in Hollywood, and I'd certainly seen my share of cross-dressers, transvestites, and transsexuals, but this was my dad. We used to come here for hot flannel cakes when I was a child. I forged my way to the brown leather booth where he had positioned himself, and put on my nicest smile like nothing was out of the ordinary. As he stood up to greet me, I said, "Hi Dad," and lightly pecked his powdered cheek.

In place of the handsome, he-man race-car driver that I remembered stood an unknown, eerie entity. As he leaned over to kiss me I smelled his familiar scent of Jack Daniel's, only this time it was mixed with a spritz of eau de gardenia. The sweet, musty odor reminded me of crumpled perfumed tissues mixed with cherry LifeSavers. He smelled like my grandmother's purse. As we sat down, he crossed his bony nylon-clad legs and daintily folded his large hands in front of him.

"Are you surprised?" he beamed.

I wasn't really sure how to respond. I think "mortified" was the feeling, but not wanting to spoil his moment, I replied, "Yep, I'm truly amazed."

My dad couldn't wait to fill me in on all the scary details of his operation. As he explained how the doctor nipped off his private parts and constructed a new vagina, I was completely lost in his shocking transformation.

He was wearing artificial, spiky, long eyelashes with iridescent blue eye shadow. He had lined his pale blue eyes with black liner and painted on the old-fashioned fishtails curling up at the ends. Dramatic, heavy brown eyebrows scrawled down to his temples, and pasty pancake foundation gave his complexion a dull, deathlike pallor. His lips were stained in a blaze of scarlet, and silver hoop earrings dangled from his large earlobes. I noticed that his gold Rolex had been replaced with the smaller female version, and feminine rings that I recognized as belonging to his late wife, Loren, were squeezed onto his swollen fingers. He held onto a fifties-style red handbag and wore matching red pumps with one wonky heel.

More strange was seeing my dad in full female regalia. He was wearing a fancy knit ensemble with a short, slim-fit skirt that showcased his stick-straight legs. To top off the whole new look, he had donned a long auburn thatch that sat slightly askew on his graying pate. The entire image was a fright.

When the waiter came to take our order, my dad suddenly developed laryngitis, and in a scratchy, high-pitched whisper ordered the grilled chops and another Jack on the rocks. My appetite had pretty much vanished when I walked in the door, but in my cheeriest tone I ordered the seafood salad and a Hires root-beer float. The waiter took off, and my dad's deep timbre suddenly came back. I guess we had fooled him; just a couple of nice girls out for an afternoon lunch.

"So what do you think? How do I look?" he gushed.

The only word I could think of was "scary," but I managed to squeak out, "Very nice, you look great, if this is what makes you happy."

My dad stared at me like I'd lost my mind and slurred, "I'm not gay, you know, I only did this so I would never be unfaithful to Loren, God rest her soul."

I was beginning to lose the plot. Wasn't this just a little excessive? I heard that a person had to go through an extensive psychiatric assessment before even being considered for this sort of procedure. It was obvious that my father was out of touch.

He went on to tell me that he had made some new friends in Palm Springs, and that they hadn't a clue that he was a transsexual. He wanted me to come out to the desert and to introduce me to these people. As what, I wondered, his daughter or her daughter? Was he supposed to be my mom now? I definitely had to draw the absurd line somewhere.

My dad liked to smoke cigarettes while he ate and now had two Lucky Strikes burning, one gripped between his fingertips and the other smoldering away in the ashtray. I noticed that he had spilled a spot of A-1 sauce on the front of his jacket, and smiled to myself re-membering how my grandfather used to tease me, saying, "Baby, you look good in everything you eat."

I passed him my napkin so he could wipe off the sauce, then tact-fully doused the extra burning butt with a teaspoon of water. I could see the booze was beginning to take effect, which always made my dad a bit maudlin and tearfully sentimental. He broke down.

"Thank God I found you, you're all I have left in the world."

He professed how much he loved me, but I wasn't biting. It was true, next to him I was the last surviving member of his family, but he'd always known exactly where to find me. It was he who had stayed away from me. I continued sipping my float to the noisy last drop, when all of a sudden he burst into tears. Something about seeing my dad cry was disarming. I had spent the last hour trying to dismiss him as a nutter, but now I felt a cold chill. There was a real person lost somewhere in there. This was the man who had given me life. I man-aged to choke out the uncomfortable words, "And I love you too."

We'd already had three different servers wait on our table, and when the fourth waiter came to bring the check I realized something was up. They were all taking turns, coming to gaze at my garishly made-up father. My dad rummaged through his red handbag and handed me a heap of credit cards held together with a rubber band. He asked me to sign the check, as he was going to go "freshen up." Everyone in the restaurant stared openly as he drunkenly tottered past their tables on his way to the powder room.

Shuffling through the lot of cards I noticed he'd already changed his name on every one of them. Even his driver's license read SEX: FE-MALE, HEIGHT: 6'4". Instead of Robert he was now Robin. It was all so shockingly official.

I started to realize that this whole transformation had been long thought out. I was pretty sure it didn't have anything to do with being faithful to Loren. If anything, he'd had to wait for her to die before he could go through with the procedure. My stepmother had been a jealous, suspicious witch. I was sure that if she had had even an inkling of this possibility, she would have divorced him and sued his pantyhose off. Hmm, she did die rather suddenly. The coroner said it was heart failure. Wow! What if he really killed her! With that frightening thought, I signed the receipt "Robin James," collected my belongings, and went to see what was taking the old girl so long in the ladies' room.

On entering I found my father leaning close to the mirror dabbing on a little more Max Factor pancake. As he applied more crimson lipstick, I had an anxious feeling, like I was about to be caught doing something I shouldn't, but what I wasn't sure. I worried that some unsuspecting female diner would breeze into the powder room and get a shock.

While my dad was taking his/her time preening in the mirror, I urgently needed to pee. I eyed the vacant stall, then looked back at his reflection in the glass. If it had been a girlfriend or even a beau with me, I wouldn't have thought twice about it, but something about my dad in the ladies' room dressed like Aunt Bea made it a little too intimate, so I decided I could hold it. Here I was in a little pink bathroom on Hollywood Boulevard watching my father put the final touches on his already overly made-up face. He took a tissue, folded it in half, and carefully blotted his lips. It was an old-fashioned technique he must have learned from observing his late wife. With one last glance in the mirror he was ready to meet the public.

I held the door open, thinking he would exit before me and I would trail inconspicuously behind, but he politely waited for me to catch up. Like a tipsy jester, he took my arm and we slowly paraded through the dining room of Musso & Frank. When we reached the exit, he stopped and waited for me to open the door, and I respectfully held it ajar. He asked if I wouldn't mind giving him a ride to his hotel, and again took my arm as we plodded to the parking lot. Seeing my little black VW convertible in the distance brought a welcome sense of reality. Not wanting to tarry, I tipped the valet a fiver and made a beeline for the Volkswagen. When we got settled in I literally breathed a sigh of relief. I glanced over at my father, who was still getting situated in the seat beside me. His knee-length skirt was hiked up to his thighs, exposing two shriveled wads of nylon lying limp between his legs. I knew they were some sort of stockings, but I wasn't sure what the extra hanging bits were. On closer inspection, I realized he was wearing two sets of pantyhose, one pair on each leg. I attempted to make sense of the strangeness, and at the same time tried not to stare as he awkwardly tugged and pulled his short skirt back over his knees. I started the car, and just as I was about to make a clean getaway, he leaned over.

"I want to show you something."

He fumbled with the brass buttons of his blazer, then proudly exposed his bare breast implants right in my face. I'd never seen an actual boob job in the flesh, but it looked like the chest of a seventeen-year-old girl joined to the head of a sixty-three-year-old blade, an original Dr. Frankenstein creation. At that moment I was officially in shock, and just about speechless. I felt like I was being assaulted but unable to defend myself. I summoned up my last shred of false enthusiasm.

"Looks like they did a great job, Dad."

Really, I was thinking, "I'd like to sue the maniac that did this to my father."

I started the car, put it in reverse, and proceeded to back straight into a solid-steel joist. I thought I had merely dented the fender, and didn't really care. I just wanted to get back to the simple solace of my own home. I put the VW in gear, but the engine just raced, and the car wouldn't budge forward or back. I climbed out and found to my horror that the bumper had somehow hooked onto the steel girder. The only way to extricate it was to lift the car or bend the chrome fender back, neither of which I could do on my own. I looked over at my dad, who was sitting demurely in the passenger's seat, and realized he had no intention of getting out to help. I'd forgotten, he was now the little lady. I glanced over at the Latin attendant who was sitting in his cash booth observing the fiasco. Fortunately, he came to my aid with a crowbar. We pushed, pried, and prodded ourselves into a sweat until the car was finally freed. I yelled a hasty thank you, gave him another fresh five, and drove off with the twisted bumper bouncing around in the backseat.

I'd just pulverized my perfect little bug, and next to me sat a completely hammered, man-sized Theda Bara. I'd been in a protective state of icy numbness most of the afternoon, but now I was beginning to thaw. My head was spinning, I needed to pee, and I felt like I was going to throw up.

I followed my dad's directions to the Hollywoodland motel, a desolate-looking shabby dive overlooking the freeway in Studio City. As we pulled into the drive, knowing he could afford better, I asked, "What made you choose this place?"

He mumbled something about not wanting to be recognized. Whatever that meant. I decided not to delve any further. We said our good-byes, and once more he asked, "Do you really think I look pretty?"

"Very nice," I reassured him, and waited as he limped off on his unsteady high heels, back to the safety of his motel room.

On the way home, for some unknown reason, my teeth started to ache, and my eyes welled up with tears. It had never occurred to me that I had a genuine emotional attachment to my father. He had always been the absent mystery man, my imaginary savior. My parents divorced when I was still a baby, and he had never really shown any sincere interest in me. Now all of a sudden he wanted to be close. I guess he needed a confidant, a girlfriend. Whatever the reason, it was all too twisted.

When I arrived home I felt like I'd been struck by a speeding loco-motive. I fell into my bed and wept big salty tears till my head felt like a saturated sponge. There's nothing like a good cry to put things into perspective. I got up, put an ice pack on my puffy eyes, and went out to Bloomingdale's to purchase my dad a new pair of sturdy high heels, size eleven.

2

My mysterious dad, the notorious ladies' man. He was a fearless, trophy-winning race-car driver, an ace pilot, and a macho stunt man. I would have believed anything about him, but not that he'd become a purse-toting, high-heeled transsexual.

When Robert came into the world his aging parents, Clarence and Helen, already had two striking lasses in their early teens. Claire was the true stunner of the family, the original bad seed with vixen green eyes and a complexion like magnolia petals. She had won the title of Miss California, and was first runner-up in the Miss America pageant of 1938. Claire and her sister, Lois, were a pair of ambitious young actresses who treated their young brother like an unwelcome weed. The three unlikely siblings battled for attention and resented each other all the way to their last failing breaths.

At the tender age of six my blond, blue-eyed dad was sent off to the austere Black Foxe Military Academy to become a man. He graduated with full honors.

As a teen his passion was building souped-up dragsters in the family four-car garage, then hot-rodding up and down the main drag of the Sunset Strip.

Robert was just seventeen when he met Diana, a narcissistic slender blonde with movie star good looks and reckless charm, a sultry, bohemian glamour girl.

At eighteen Diana was way ahead of her time. She was already experimenting with peyote, puffing reefer, and dropping amphetamines like lemon drops. She was the unlikely young woman who would share in giving me life.

My parents met at Beverly Hills High School, and Robert was quickly besotted with her wild way. He'd circle her house on Palm Drive like a feisty young tom, laying smokin' rubber well into the night. He eventually got her attention and they went for a spin, and ended up getting married in a chapel in Mexico. With no place of their own they moved into the guest quarters of my dad's family residence, a two-story Mediterranean, high above Sunset with a breathtaking view of all of Los Angeles. On a clear day you could see as far as Catalina Island from the verandah.

I arrived with a cheerful disposition during the full moon on May 31, 1950. Unfortunately the novelty of my parents' teen marriage was already waning. Some of my early memories are slightly hazy, but most of it sticks in my head like bright colored Polaroids. I easily recall the perpetual drama in our house; my young parents fought like rabid dogs going for the kill. I'd often lie awake at night listening to a cacophony of breaking furniture, shattering glass, and horror show screams wailing through the halls. My parents chased each other with daggers and shoved each other about and down the stairs. From the upstairs window I often saw whirling red lights from the squad cars that arrived at our neighbor's request. Usually my grandparents smoothed it over with the West Hollywood sheriffs, but all too often my deflated dad would be hauled off in handcuffs.

My last night in my grandparents' home, my dad, who smelled like a cocktail lounge, yanked me out of bed, and we hightailed it down to his beloved red Caddy parked in the drive. We locked the doors but Diana was close behind, wielding a stiletto blade. In an abandoned rage, she flailed at the windows, jumped up on the hood, and slashed the soft ragtop of my dad's Cadillac to shreds.

The next thing I knew, without any explanation, I was being sent away to an unknown abode. My grandmother James packed a small suitcase, and the two of us drove to a most extraordinary house in downtown Los Angeles. The place was an enormous four-story Victorian mansion sitting on a slope off a wide sumptuous avenue. This elegant neighborhood was the once affluent Adams district. The historic residence, called "Kiddy College California," was like a turn-of-the-century boarding school, privately owned and run by an elderly couple, Mr. and Mrs. March.

Mrs. March was slight and ailing, a wisp of a woman with a snow-white braid perfectly coiled and neatly pinned around her shrinking head. She was all but lost, propped up in layers of feather-down pillows. Her marble-top nightstand was overflowing with an assortment of vials, pills, and interesting-looking amber tinctures. In a deliberate drawl she forewarned, "Children should be seen and not heard."

I was only four years old, but it was clear that Mrs. March and I weren't going to be friends.

Although the old girl was frail, she still possessed a strict, authoritarian shrill that could be heard two floors down. She mostly ruled the roost from her ornate Edwardian bed, but on rare occasions she'd stroll the dorms in her ghostly white nightgown and give all the children a fright. Some nights, after checking her wards, she'd stand in front of the oval mirror in the dormitory and pluck the tan tortoise-shell pins from her tightly wrapped braid. Her hair was so long that the plait would unravel like a coiled rope and hit the carpet with a soft thump. I wondered if my hair would ever grow that long. If it did, I would wear it exactly like Mrs. March.

Schooling took place in a detached building on the estate that appeared to be a small theater. It had an elevated stage that spanned the length of the room. This is where the girls learned to curtsy and the boys became proficient in folding the American flag. If the Stars and Stripes even brushed the floor it would have to be kissed or else burned. We sat in tight rows of wooden desks, and you'd better not be caught slumping, or you'd spend the rest of the day standing and holding a broomstick vertically across your back to keep your posture straight. And none of us escaped the dunce cap. If we were called upon in class and lacked a satisfactory reply, we were made to sit on a stool, center stage, wearing the tall pointy red dunce cone while the other kids sang a humbling little ditty they called "The Sad Little Tomato."

When school let out we were free to roam the pastoral fairyland gardens. There was a grand pond teeming with squishy fat bullfrogs and fragrant bushes of anise where ladybugs thrived. I delighted in catching the gentle orange bugs. I'd put them in a glass jar with a sprig of green and hide them deep in the briar and catch more the next day. On warm summer weekends the kids who didn't go home were allowed to frolic, and to cool off in the front-yard sprinklers till the sun set.

Along with Mr. and Mrs. March there was a small staff of three. Miss Owen was the heavyset schoolmarm who walked with a limp and labored for breath. She wore flesh-tone stockings that matted the coarse hair of her legs into swirling, spidery patterns. Her fleshy hands always smelled like fish cakes, and she wore a shiny silver thimble on her middle finger. She took pleasure in creeping up behind us in class and bonking the top of our innocent heads with the metal device, making sure we were alert and paying attention.

Lizzy was the rail-thin black woman who did house chores and tenderly bathed the children every Saturday. Lizzy would lather me up in sweet-smelling baby soap, then rinse me down with a warm, handheld shower hose. She called the water on my pink skin "raindrops."

"Be still, baby girl, we got to catch all them raindrops." And she'd gently pat me dry with a soft white flannel.

Her husband, Old John, was the handyman who repaired broken windows and squeaky doors. He was also the gardener, and kept the extensive grounds and gardens flourishing. He was quite the character in his Farmer John overalls and wide-brim straw hat, a dead ringer for the old gent in *Song of the South*.

Our schoolmistress, Miss Owen, lodged in an apartment directly upstairs from the classroom. If the children got too boisterous while she was taking her afternoon rest, she'd lean out of her second-story window and douse us with a bucket of cold water, and we'd all squeal and scatter off to the pond to chase the bullfrogs.

I got along at the home okay, but I suffered from recurrent nightmares. I'd always dream that I was being kidnapped by strangers or that I'd be lost on a desolate street. I also had a fear of the dark. When the lights went out, and the other children were asleep, I saw armies of imaginary king-sized insects crawling on my bedsheets and covers. I got so terrified I'd often wet the bed. When old Mrs. March got word of the bed-wetting I was summoned to her room. Lizzy led me to the foot of her bedstead, then abandoned me to the fury of the missus. Trying to avoid her angry glare, I concentrated hard on the pattern of pink florets on my damp flannel nightdress. Mrs. March, with no warning, took a full glass of water from her nightstand and flung it straight into my scared, repentant face. As I stood stunned in my wetness, she said, "I've heard you like to be wet." Then she waved her hand toward the door, scowling. "You may be dismissed."

I hated the old crone and only wished I could go back to my family. I wondered if my parents even knew where I was or if my grandmother had forgotten where she had left me. I don't remember how long I lived at the school, but one morning while I was collecting my ladybugs, I was called up to the parlor. It was my dad's mother, Helen, my grandmother James. She was holding my little suitcase. I was finally going home.

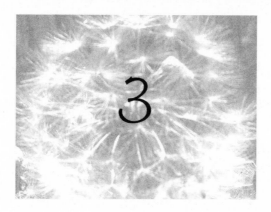

1 wouldn't be going back to the big house on Ozeta Terrace. My grandmother James said my parents didn't live together any-more, and that I'd be living in a new house with my mother.

Diana had moved into a small 1920s bungalow apartment just a few blocks away, below Sunset. My erratic, twenty-two-year-old mother was now on her own, and even though she was saddled with a four-year-old daughter, it didn't seem to slow her down.

My mother stayed out most nights with an array of handsome, hopeful suitors. I'd watch in devotion as she got dolled up for a night on the town. She'd swoop her blond mane into a carefree twist, and smudge her pretty lips with fiery red. In the mirror she'd flip up her collar in that cool fifties way, and slather on creamy hand lotion that smelled like fresh tuberose. Then she'd be off to check out Lenny Bruce at the Unicorn or slip across Sunset to her friend Mickey's jazz club, the Renaissance, which is now the House of Blues, for some late-night Miles Davis. On the rare occasion she took me along, I'd fall asleep in the smoky light booth upstairs to the dizzying sounds of jumpin' jazz. When she left me home alone, I'd be under strict orders: "Do not answer the phone or open the door to anyone."

She'd serve me my usual little bowl of Farina or Cream of Wheat, switch on the television set, and be gone like the wind, leaving a lingering trail of her lovely perfume wafting in the air.

Like a bored puppy I found plenty of mischief to get into. One night I passed the evening painting the bottom half of the walls with coal-black boot polish. Another night I played with the electric mixer till I got my little fingers stuck in the spinning prongs. When I found the scissors and cut the front of my hair like she did (except I cut mine to the scalp) my mother decided I could no longer be left to my own devices.

Now whenever Diana went out she'd sit me in front of the television set and secure me to a wooden chair with one of her wide leather belts. She'd fastened the strap around my waist and buckle it taut to the back of the seat, then tie my feet to the legs with extension cords. The last TV show of the night was the news with George Putnam. At the end of each show George would say, "That's the news at ten, I'll see you then." Then he'd give a firm patriotic salute. When "The Star-Spangled Banner" followed I felt uneasy, because I was completely alone. I'd eventually doze off to the drone of the Indian head TV test pattern. When she got home she'd unfasten the cinches, and I'd scurry to my spot on the sofa. In the morning I feasted on bits of steak and squishy desserts from whatever fancy restaurant she had dined at the night before. This was our dreary routine.

One night I squirmed my way out of the chair and toddled out the front door, which closed behind me and locked me out of the apartment. A neighbor heard me crying in the late-night air and took me in till Diana returned home from the Sunset Strip. From then on I slept in a dinky locked closet in the hallway.

Curled up in the dark, on top of Diana's entangled mound of spiky heels, with crowded clothing suspended over my head, I heard the sounds of heavy, alternating crashing waves and had the feeling I was about to drown. Then a faint choir of angels began singing in my ears. I could even see angel silhouettes floating in the darkness. I hadn't yet been exposed to religion, but I had an innate sense of God, and knew I came from someplace better. I prayed to go to sleep and never wake up; I wanted to go back to heaven. I closed my eyes tight, ready for takeoff. After what seemed like hours I'd take squinty, hopeful peeks in the dark, but still only felt the hems of my mother's coats and dresses resting on my head.

My mother took sleeping pills that knocked her out cold, and she slept deep as the dead with a classical radio station turned down low until midafternoons. For hours on end I'd stand silent and still by her four-poster bed, waiting, watching for the slightest sign of life. Just the faintest quiver of her finger would put my baby heart at ease, and I thanked God she was still alive. I'd tiptoe back to the kitchen, climb up on the stool, and whisper to Al, "It's okay, she's still breathing."

Al was our miniature pet turtle who lived in a clear plastic tureen of water with a dwarf palm tree in the center. He'd pop out his tiny spotted head and we'd have long, meaningful conversations. Al was a stunning listener. When my turtle mysteriously vanished from his dish one morning, never to be seen again, there was no longer anyone to confide in, and my house felt gravely lonely. I searched every corner of our apartment but never did find out what happened to Al.

When my mother got a new boyfriend sometimes she wouldn't come home all night. On New Year's Eve she found a couple of babysitters in the classifieds, and she and I went for a long drive, deep into the San Fernando Valley.

My sitters were a pair of white-haired spinster sisters trying to make a little extra cash on the side. I don't remember their names, but the older of the two was blind, half deaf, and bedridden. Her stagnant room was decked out like a hospital, rigged with IVs, oxygen tanks, and an assortment of walking aids. I could smell the piney scent of disinfectant mingled with the distinct odor of stale urine. Her short-tempered sister was the reluctant nursemaid, and also hard of hearing. She spoke to me in a blaring screech that hurt my sensitive ears. They were an interesting duet, but it was not the ideal environment for a five-year-old. The plan was for me to stay overnight, and my mother would collect me in the morning. We watched the entire New Year's Day parade on their black-and-white Philco, and my mom still hadn't called or shown up. I could sense the woman was becoming agitated.

"Where is your mother?" she snarled. "Ya know, I can't have you here all day!"

She'd been had, and I had the familiar feeling my mother wasn't coming back. The weary old girl had her hands full changing bedpans and IVs, and now she had a child to wrangle with.

For the next few days, while she ate Swanson TV dinners, she fed me a diet of canned beans and cornflakes. She also took to pulling me around the house by my hair. I'd complain, "Ouch, you're pulling my hair."

She'd snap back, "I'm not pulling your hair, dearie, you're just trying to get away."

I tried standing perfectly still, but I'm certain she was yanking my locks on purpose.

After trying to figure out what to do with me, the three of us packed into their old model tanker, oxygen rig in tow. The old nags dropped me off at MacClaren Hall, a kiddy pokey for lost ragamuffins and unwanted waifs.

I didn't miss staying with the crusty sisters. I was happy back in a dormitory just like at Mrs. March's, with rows of iron beds and other children to play with. Unlike at my mother's house, the mornings were cheerful, no dark closets, tiptoeing, or monitoring for vital signs. There was a routine, a reassuring, comforting order. After chores the children would line up single file and march off to the dining hall. Aluminum platters heaped with warm scrambled eggs and stacks of buttered toast were served on long tables. The afternoons passed happily in the dayroom with cupboards of old toys and well-loved dolls. I wanted to stay there forever.

Late one night I was awakened abruptly, dressed, and taken down a long corridor to the admissions office because someone had come to see me. Waiting in reception was a radiant blond woman dressed in a black overcoat and stiletto high heels. I could smell her powdery Shalimar perfume all the way down the hall. The lady had a gentle smile, and was holding out a brand-new baby doll. This charismatic creature was my eccentric maternal grandmother.

At forty-nine she was still a stunning dish, with flawless powder-puff skin and luminous green eyes. Her glossy black '55 Lincoln was waiting out front for my getaway.

Her name was Evelyn, but for an unknown reason I called her Mimi. Throughout the rest of my life, Mimi would be my guardian angel. I never knew how she found me, but from that moment on, she was always there to rescue me.

Mimi lived with my grandfather Albert in a stately residence in the Hollywood flatlands. Al was a towering, blond German with two missing fingers who played the boogie-woogie like he'd invented it. I'd sit on his lap while he played, and it felt like the piano was about to take to the air. He'd make the whole house rock with his soulful music. Albert Newman played with the big-band leaders Abe Lyman and Phil Harris. He also orchestrated films at RKO and 20th Century–Fox for the likes of Al Jolson, Fred Astaire, and Bing Crosby. My grandparents' home was always filled with music and parades of actors. I remember being mesmerized by gangster matinee idol George Raft, who I'm sure charmed the pants off all the pretty girls of his time. He had an elegant, impeccable style with a delightful glint of danger in his eyes—one of the original Hollywood bad boys. The first time I encountered Mr. Raft was during breakfast with my grandparents at the Beverly Wilshire Hotel coffee shop. I fell in love with a life-sized stuffed standard poodle in the gift display that was big enough to ride. Mimi said I couldn't have the pooch, but Mr. Raft plucked the dog from the counter and set the furry black hound in my arms. After that morning he never came to visit without a gracious gift in hand.

The Marx Brothers were regular visitors, and I called each one "Uncle." Harpo was my favorite. Once I was backstage with my grandparents at one of their charity revues when Harpo picked me up and perched me on his lap. As he was speaking to my grandfather I noticed something curious about his hair. There were odd metal pins peeking out from his temples. I gently tugged at a section of curls and the whole curly wig slipped off in my hand. He looked as surprised as I was.

"Oh no no, don't do that," he whispered, then swiftly slipped the wig back in place. Harpo and Chico would pretend to fight over which one of them would marry me when I grew up. After serious deliberation I realized it was only fair to choose uncle Harpo, as he'd been the one who had asked me first. My future was secure: When I was old enough I'd become Mrs. Harpo Marx.

My Mimi had a romantic nature, and a high sense of drama. She was a gifted healer and an amazingly accurate psychic. She taught me the mysteries of numerology, palm reading, and how to interpret the Tarot cards. She once solemnly confided that we were from another planet, which I never questioned. We often went for long drives in the country and stopped in fragrant orange groves to picnic on lemon tarts and fresh raspberries. She read and recited poetry to me in her loving, soothing tone. My favorite was "The Dandelion."

Oh Dandelion yellow as gold, what do you do all day?
I just sit here in the tall green grass 'til my hair grows old and gray.
Dandelion, what do you do when your hair turns long and white?
I sway in the tall green grass 'til the children come to play.
They pick me up in their little hands and blow my hair away.

Her words were like pictures that came to life. I lived each and every story, and loved the lilt of the rhyme. She knew the names of every blossom and flower of the wayside, and our special favorite was the delicate face of the pansy. Mimi loved Mozart and Chopin, but most of all she relished the quiet. Usually after my grandfather left for the movie studio, we'd get ready to go on one of our dreamy little outings. One morning I was so excited to go, I was bouncing on her white silk sofa like a whirling dervish. When I ignored her requests to settle down, she sighed, put her hand to her heart, and fell dead to the carpet. She definitely had my attention. I leaped off the couch, leaned over her still body, and whispered, "Mimi, Mimi." I tugged on her hand, but she was lifeless. I thought I had killed her. I quickly turned on my Cinderella record player and put on the yellow vinyl "Dance of the Sugar Plum Fairies." I turned the volume to high, and danced around her still body Isadora Duncan style, hoping to revive her. I believed classical music had something to do with heaven and would bring her back to life. After several airy pirouettes and graceful leaps, my appeal was heard, and she miraculously awoke, and all was forgiven. Mimi was as dramatic as she was original.

Mimi enrolled me in the Beverly Hills Catholic School, where I learned to spell Catherine, and got to play the part of an angel in the Christmas play. I instantly loved Catholic school. I liked the clear, crisp order, and I finally knew what was expected of me. I was born with an overdose of spirituality, and at the school it was revealed in living color. The holy spirit wasn't just in my head, he lived here. I loved the sacred splendor of the church and felt a deep affinity with the blessed weeping statues of Jesus and the Virgin. I was in awe of the Father, the Son, and Holy Ghost, and mesmerized by halos, holy water, the crucifix, and the taking of sacrament. I wanted to be a nun like the mother superior, wearing the golden wedding band and flowing hallowed habit. When I grew up I wanted to be married to Jesus.

I hadn't seen or heard from my mother for almost two years, not since the day she dropped me off with the old girls in the San Fernando Valley. Meanwhile, she'd remarried and given birth to a new baby. One day, without warning, Diana decided it was time to reclaim me. Most likely she wanted me back because she needed someone to look after her newborn. My Mimi didn't give me up without a fight. They each grabbed one of my limbs and pulled me like a tug-of-war rope in and out of the front door. In the midst of the jumble, neither of them realized they were about to yank my arms clean out. Mimi finally lost her grip, and my mother dragged me off to the car shouting, "You'll never see this child again!"

In my eyes Mimi was my mother. Living with Diana was lonely, and I was afraid of her. The thought of never seeing Mimi again was shattering, but I got in the car without a peep.

Diana's new husband, Jack, was a good-looking twenty-three-year-old kid from a well-to-do family in Beverly Hills. I didn't know much about him, except that he drove a fancy English sports car called a Doretti and worked as a salesman at his parents' car dealership in Beverly Hills. I think he also sold marijuana as a sideline. He seemed to be a bit of a beatnik, and just adventurous enough to be attracted to Diana's dangerous flame. My mother demanded I address her new groom as "Uncle Daddy," but there was something about that dismal title that stuck in my throat like a soiled mop. I barely knew this man; he wasn't my uncle or my daddy. I had to close my eyes and make myself invisible just to utter the cryptic words.

I was only seven years on the earth and had already lived in six different extraordinary environments—and had two fathers. First it was bedlam at my real dad's house on Ozeta Terrace, then the boarding school with cadaverous Mrs. March. There was my stint with Diana in Hollywood, and on to the old babysitting bats in the valley. Mac-Claren Hall was most comforting, but Mimi and Al were my first real family. Now all of a sudden I had a new uncle and was responsible for my infant brother.

In a short time I learned to change diapers, sterilize bottles, and feed a baby. Except for the routine care, Diana and Uncle Daddy appeared to love their new son. They coddled, pampered, and cooed over little Scot, and rarely went anywhere without taking him along. As for me, I felt like an apparition from the distant past. My mother barely acknowledged my presence, and rarely fed me. Uncle Daddy was nice enough, but he never stepped in between me and my mother. When she was sleeping I'd feed myself from the sugar bowl, being careful not to have too much, so she would not notice it was gone. She again took to tying me in a chair or locking me in my bedroom before leaving the house. For a bit of company I talked to my doll, who had matted brown curls and an understanding expression. I'd tell her,

"When I grow up I'm going to have a baby and treat it really good." The doll stared back like she was absorbed in every word. I was sure she could hear me, and thought there must be a secret doll pact where they weren't allowed to speak.

One night after my parents left the house I heard a light tap on my bedroom window, and a familiar voice whispering outside: "It's Mimi, love."

It was my grandmother—she'd waited down the block till the coast was clear, and risked the wrath of Diana to see me. Mimi was the only human I'd ever felt an attachment to, and the only one who showed me softness. Just the sound of her gentle voice put my confused heart at ease. She brought me peanut butter sandwiches and a package of fluffy pink Hostess snowballs that she passed under the slightly opened window. From then on my grandparents came on a regular basis. Mimi would bring food and talk with me from the bushes while my grandfather kept watch at the driveway. That's how I got to see my grandparents: secretively, through a crack in the window.

My mother's second marriage was not unlike the previous disaster with my real father. In the beginning their marriage looked like a slice of American pie. Diana and Jack were a glamorous couple with a new baby, a new house, a white Chrysler Imperial convertible in the driveway, and Uncle Daddy started a thriving car dealership of his own. My mother could have lived the life of Riley, but as usual there was trouble in paradise. It was the same constant conflict and late-night brawls as at my real father's house. Diana was never content until she'd dissected and destroyed everything in her reach.

One night Uncle Daddy awoke from a deep sleep and found that Diana was not in their bed, or anywhere else in the house. The next night he lay in wait and discovered that his dauntless young bride had actually been dosing his merlot with knockout pills, then slipping out for the night. As bewitching and beautiful as she appeared, Jack was no match for my untamed mother. Their ill-fated union lasted less than four years.

We made a hasty retreat from prestigious Brentwood back to Hollywood, and the three of us settled into a two-story Craftsman house on Harriet Street, a block below Sunset.

Our mother still slept till the crack of noon or later, and kept the phone off the hook. It was my post to keep our house clean, and to make sure my four-year-old brother didn't make a peep. If Scot made the slightest sound that woke her I'd be in double trouble.

At eleven years old I was already a gangly five-foot-six inches, with long blond hair and no perception of my blossoming allure. My mother regularly reproached me: "Just look at yourself! How could you have come from me?"

I was sorry to be such an unsatisfactory burden to her, but unfortunately that was something neither of us had the power to change.

Diana was a fascinating dichotomy. Besides her obvious outward beauty and reckless charm, she was a gifted writer, a sultry singer, and she played an array of instruments. She even recorded a bluegrass album for Elektra records. She was also a talented artist who could meticulously copy any piece of art to the letter. She would have made a brilliant forger. Everything she attempted seemed to come effortlessly and turn out flawless. She was also shockingly selfish and rarely spoke without mean-spirited sarcasm.

My mother was a true narcissist and often almost psychotic. Her drug addiction didn't help matters. She downed hefty doses of uppers, downers, and any kind of painkillers she could get her hands on. I don't think I ever saw her when she wasn't under the influence of some nerve-deadening narcotic. She called her poison "vitamins," and kept her stash in an orderly antique black doctor's bag.

Along with my mother's other numerous talents, she was also an industrious cat burglar who believed anything and everything was hers for the taking. She would peruse the obituaries, then case the addresses of the deceased. In the late night Miss Diana would take me and my little brother along as accomplices. She'd look for unlocked windows and boost me or Scot up into the casements of strange houses so we could get in and unlock the doors. While our mother pillaged the residences for antiques and other items of value, one of us kept a lookout. She even carried off the glass doorknobs and lighting fixtures. She would have taken the crown molding if she could have got to it. When she got what she had come for we would help her load her car with the spoils. There wasn't a doubt in my mind that what we were doing was wrong, but it was out of the question to question my mother. While touring the 160-room historic Winchester House in San Jose, she actually lifted the lace Victorian linens clean off the bed. She also pillaged any unsecured garage, and had no ethics when she had access to someone's medicine cabinet. My mother was a brazen bandit.

Aside from her lawless ways, I was mystified by Diana's attractiveness and accomplishments. I thought she was the all-knowing goddess, and was both in awe and afraid of her. Perhaps I wasn't as pretty or as clever as she, but she did her best to make sure I wouldn't catch up. She dressed me in ungainly, oversized hand-me-downs, and my only pair of shoes looked like prewar issue. Each week Diana would check the lumpish heels to make sure they were wearing exactly in the middle. If the rear of the heel showed the least bit of wear to the side, she'd say I walked like "the low class," and threatened to give the ugly clown-toed oxfords to a girl who was more appreciative, a girl who knew how to walk like a young lady. Besides the shoe ordinance, there was to be no sweating, audible breathing, or speaking unless spoken to allowed in her presence. I was now also to address her as "ma'am."

There were frequent all-night parties at our house on Harriet, and you could just about suffocate in the clouds of marijuana. Sometimes my mother and her arriving passengers would brew up a musty-smelling, deep kettle of psychedelic peyote buttons, and they'd all trip out till dawn. In the morning our living room looked like the aftermath of the Civil War, with bodies crashed out wherever they fell.

Occasionally one of the party suspects would stumble into my bedroom for a late-night chat. I'd awake to some would-be pervert trying to stroke my hair in the dark while whispering sexual indecencies close to my ear. The notion of oral copulation gave me the creeps; surely no one actually did anything as wicked as that. There was one wanton maniac who was most persistent, and professed his inane love for me, vowing to wait till I was ready. Ready for what? I had no idea what anyone was talking about, and thankfully managed to fend off their twisted desires.

Although my mother never once said she loved me, or touched me without rage, I wasn't deterred. I never stopped trying to win her affection. I kept our house immaculate, washed and ironed her clothes, and had her coffee ready when she woke up in the afternoon. Still, no matter how hard I tried to please her, she either shunned or scorned me.

I had a glimmer of hope when she admired an extravagant inkwell at a ritzy antique shop on Melrose Avenue. Each day while she was sleeping, I'd take little Scot and canvass our neighborhood. I'd ask the neighbors if I might wash their dishes, polish their cars, or rake their leaves, anything I could do to earn forty dollars and procure that inkwell. I thought giving her something so grand would surely soften her bitterness and magically make her love me. I saved the whole summer long, hiding the singles and multitude of silver change in a cigar box under my bed. I was joyous just imagining how impressed she might be with her industrious daughter.

I finally earned the ransom, and wrapped the bronze cast in white stationery paper and tied it with a single strand of pink ribbon.

Usually when Diana woke up I'd shudder with dread. She'd shout

"Catherine!" at the top of her lungs like Satan had risen and I'd rush up the stairs with a peace offering cup of coffee. She liked her brew extra sweet, laden with cream, and I'd deliver it to her bed while she interrogated me like a provoked drill sergeant.

"What have you been doing, where is your brother, have you cleaned the house?"

Today she'd have a special surprise. I set the tray with her coffee, and my devoted offering, on the edge of her bed and waited with hopeful anticipation. Diana unwrapped my package like it was drenched in cooties.

"How did you get this?"

I explained how I'd worked all summer and earned the money for it. There was a silent pause, then her words of wisdom hit me like a crashing wave.

"That's nice, Catherine, but here's a lesson for you: Love cannot be bought."

My mother was relentless. I had tried everything I knew to get her attention and win her love. But she was right: I'd resorted to bribery.

Another of Diana's odd eccentricities was that she'd go on mysterious little trips. I never knew when she was leaving or when she was coming home. I'd wake up in the morning and she'd be long gone. No note, no nothing but some leftover food in the fridge. She'd often be gone for an entire week, leaving us alone—and me to take care of my three-year-old brother. I'd become accustomed to the unpredictable, but not knowing where she was or if she was ever coming back was unsettling. I was used to taking care of Scot and looking after our house, but during one of her jaunts I had a scary accident. I was making Scot's breakfast and used the iron skillet that Diana stored bacon fat in on the stove. The fat got too hot and was beginning to smoke, so I pushed the pan to the back burner. As I moved it the grease took on a life of its own and jumped out of the pan in one big surge. The smoking fat hit me plumb in the face, and I heard my flesh sizzling like fresh bacon. I covered my face with a dishcloth, but when I took the towel away half of my skin went with it. The next day my whole face had puffed up like charred marshmallows. It blistered into alarming crispy black puffs all over my face, and there was no way to hide it. I wasn't as worried about myself as I was about what Diana would do when she saw me. I looked like a serious burn victim, but when she got home she barely noticed. All she said was, "I want to know why God punished you." This was my mother.

We lived just a block away from the West Hollywood elementary school. My mother was never up early enough to register me, so I took it upon myself to enroll in fifth grade. One afternoon during recess I fell on the playground and felt a painful snap at my wrist. The school nurse thought my arm might be broken and sent me home with a note recommending I be taken to see a doctor. My mother was infuriated by the letter.

"How dare you complain at school! God is punishing you because you don't deserve to go to school."

Diana was hardly a religious woman, but she used God to disguise her unwavering meanness. Whenever I was sick or got hurt she'd tell me to think about why God was punishing me. I didn't believe God was punishing me; I knew it was her.

I'd been blessed with vivid spiritual dreams since I was old enough to remember. I once dreamed I was sitting by a river talking with Jesus. He held my hand and gently placed something in my palm. It was a simple golden key. Jesus didn't say what it was for, but I intrinsically sensed he was entrusting me with something powerful. It was my sacred dreams that gave me an inner peace, and the strength to deflect Diana's caustic daggers. I continue to carry the golden key, and it's never let me down.

By nightfall my limb and fingers had swollen into an aching shade of blue and throbbed to the rhythm of my heart. Still she refused to even look, maintaining there was nothing wrong with my arm. I asked her permission to soak it in water.

"Yes, you may, after you've finish doing the ironing."

A week later, when I hadn't returned to school, two policemen and a gent from the health department came banging on our front door. I peeked out and whispered, "My mother's sleeping."

"Well then, we'll go wake her up," they said, pushing past me.

The idea of uniformed policemen tromping up to my mother's bedroom just couldn't happen. I quietly spoke, "No, wait here, I'll get her."

I tiptoed up the old staircase that always creaked when I was trying to be quiet, and stood close to her creamy, tucked-satin headboard. She was as still as death, with her heavy black eyeliner smudged and caked from the night before. She looked mean even in her sleep. I got up my courage: "Mother, the police are here."

I thanked Jesus that she hadn't heard me, and stood like a trapped mouse trying to think of an escape. The *police* were downstairs in our living room because of me; my life was definitely about to be over. I couldn't bring myself to wake the rage, so I crept back down the stairs, deciding to tell the cops she wasn't home. As luck would have it, a friend of my mother's and one of my midnight suitors, Richard, had stopped by, and was chatting with the sheriffs. I don't know what he said, but the officials left without further ado.

Her friend Richard was a nightclub owner. I'm guessing he was in his twenties, or maybe early thirties. He wasn't a bad-looking guy, skinny as a beanpole with curly brown hair, and pleasant enough. He lived in Hollywood not far from our house, and tooled around town in a silver Austin Healy. Aside from his ill fetish for schoolgirls he seemed genuinely concerned about my arm. I disregarded his prior late-night indiscretions and was thankful to be going to a doctor. He packed me into his two-seater and, at his own expense, took me to his personal physician.

Dr. Pobiers in Beverly Hills took some X-rays, and sure enough it was broken to the bone and already beginning to mend. It was too swollen to put in a cast and would have to be kept on ice overnight, till the swelling came down. It was clearly something Diana wasn't about to do, so it was Richard's lucky day; he was free to take his jailbait back to his bachelor pad, no questions asked. He made up a bed for me on his couch and gently wrapped my arm in ice compresses throughout the night.

The next day Dr. Pobiers patched my arm in fresh white plaster. I was proud of my chalky white cast. It reinforced my belief that I wasn't delusional, as my mother had maintained. My wrist had definitely been broken, and if it hadn't been for the luck of Richard, my hand would have mended with a permanent crook.

I continued to stay with my new benefactor, and my mother never even called or questioned where I was.

Richard delighted in taking me shopping for fancy new school dresses, and we exchanged my bumbling brown oxfords for a more stylish pair of pink, feminine flats. We'd go to the movies, cruise the arcade in Santa Monica, play skee-ball—and do anything else an eleven-year-old girl with a cast on her arm wanted to do. He'd drive me to school in the mornings and give me lunch money, a whole dollar, even though the cafeteria meal was only thirty-five cents. At the three o'clock bell Richard would be in front of West Hollywood Elementary, hunkered in his sports car waiting to take me back to his lair. I referred to Richard as my stepfather and thought it was all on the up-and-up. There weren't any more sexual overtones, at least none I couldn't avert or make light of. Later, as a grown woman, I recognized that the relationship was hot off the steamy pages of *Lolita*.

Richard was obsessed with the ocean and owned a forty-seven-foot sailboat that he docked in Marina Del Rey. One day he took me out sailing. He was going to teach me the ropes of high-sea adventure. After a long day of surf and sun, on the way back to Hollywood, I fell fast asleep in the two-seater. I awoke to find a disturbing, rough hand inching its way up my cotton summer dress and getting way too close to my panties. I pushed his hand away. Richard blurted, "Don't you understand, I'm in love with you!"

He went on to say that we could sail to Tahiti, where it was common for eleven-year-old girls to marry, and that no one would ever find us there. I understood the essence of what he was saying, but couldn't comprehend the full concept. He was speaking to me like I was a woman, but I hadn't had enough life experience to understand the emotion behind the words. I was just a kid, and he was scaring me. As a distraction I turned on the transistor radio he had bought me and held it close to my ear. I blew big pink bubbles with the juicy wad of Double Bubble in my mouth, trying to pretend this wasn't happening, but Richard floored the gas pedal.

"Damn you, Catherine, if you don't put that radio down and listen to me, I'm gonna crash this car straight into a wall. I promise I'll kill us both!"

I set the radio in my lap and stared out the passenger window while he raved on. The jig was up, he wasn't my stepfather, and I couldn't stay at his house anymore. When we came to a stoplight I jumped out of the car in the middle of traffic on Sunset, and ran. I didn't want to go back to my mother's house; there had to be someplace to go where someone rational loved me. The only place I could think of was my real father's house.

I hadn't seen my father in seven years, since I was four, but still remembered my way to Ozeta Terrace. I walked the Sunset Strip all the way from Beverly Hills, past Doheny, and finally arrived at the big house on top of the hill.

There they were, the same two old Cadillacs still parked in the garage. The grand old Spanish house with its tiled roof, wrought-iron

gates, and perfectly manicured rolling front lawn looked just as I'd remembered. I walked the extended brick steps leading to the front door
and was greeted by my glamorous aunt Claire. The statuesque Claire
was as always, dressed to attract. She stood in the doorway wearing a
figure-hugging calf-length black jersey dress with a single strand of
long pearls and a black wide-brim hat with a red silk rose.

Aunt Claire, my dad's older sister, was one of the many girls who
auditioned for the role of Scarlett O'Hara in *Gone with the Wind*. Although she didn't get the part she did have a speaking cameo with
Vivien Leigh. She'd been married to the famous choreographer Busby
Berkeley, in addition to having been Miss California. She had also
been a Ziegfeld girl who still lived in the old glory days.

"Your father doesn't live here anymore," she said. "He's remarried."

Still, Claire invited me in and offered to call him at his new home.
Nothing in the old house had changed. It was as though time had
stood still. My grandparents had bought the house new in 1930, and it
had never been redecorated.

I waited in the elegant living room, sitting straight with my feet together on the cushy rose velvet sofa. This beautiful room, with its
floor-to-ceiling arched French windows, now had an eerie stillness.
The weighty green curtains were drawn and laden with years of dust.
The once vivid Deco carpets were worn and fading. Over the fireplace
hung a life-sized oil portrait of Claire, which easily could have been
mistaken for the beautiful actress Gene Tierney. Below her canvas sat
the old mantel clock, gently clicking off the seconds, but the quarter-
hour Westminster chimes sounded sorrowful and slightly out of tune.
The ebony piano was covered with dusty family pictures and beauty
pageant trophies from a happier time. It felt like the place was slowly
rotting.

As I gazed at the life-sized portrait of my boyish father in his military school dress uniform I realized he was a mystery to me. I hoped

he'd be happy I was here, and wondered, had he missed me as much as I missed him?

My surprise visit had caused a bit of a stir. While Claire frantically tried to locate my dad, I wandered about the house reminiscing about my childhood memories.

I heard a symphony of ticking sounds and traced the clamor down the hall to where my grandparents used to sleep. The room was almost breathing with a profusion of alarm clocks. They were of every ilk and era and covered every flat surface of the room. There were at least a hundred timepieces, all click-clacking in bizarre unison.

There were the old matching high beds, still covered with the same dusty pink embroidered satin coverlets. By the window were two wide chests of drawers, obscured by clocks and separated by the shredding, pale-pink fainting couch.

Since my mother and I left there had been a changing of the guard. My grandfather, Clarence, had died of heart failure and Aunt Claire, having been divorced for the third time, had moved back into the house with her son, Blake. Blake was my cousin and we were the same age. We used to play and share the dayroom here when we were toddlers. Like my father, he attended Black Foxe Military Academy, and liked to march around in his dress uniform. Claire still worked as a day player in the movies and employed the clocks to be sure she'd rise for her five A.M. call. She was still wildly eccentric.

I heard the roar of my dad's '59 Corvette charging up Ozeta Terrace. For seven child years I had dreamed of this moment. He jumped out of his roadster and squeezed me almost too tight. With tears in his eyes, he gushed, "You're coming with me, I'm taking you home."

As he hugged me, I remembered his scent, his hair, his clothes, the smell of his breath. He smelled just the same as when I was a little girl: soft baby powder; engine fumes with a hint of distilled spirits on his lips.

We sped up Mulholland Drive and turned onto a steep hill leading to his home.

"Wait in the car for a minute," my dad said.

I heard shouting. It seemed that he hadn't mentioned to his wife that I was coming along, and she wasn't exactly delighted.

Loren was a bit of a plain Jane my dad had dated at Beverly Hills High. When he met my mother he had dropped Loren like a live grenade. After my parents divorced she won him back, but made sure he carried the cross. My existence was a sorry reminder of his early indiscretion and the subject of bitter contention.

What Loren lacked in beauty, she made up for with style and a sarcastic disposition. She was as thin as a rail, with boyish, cropped, bleached hair. She wore her crisp white blouse with the collar up and tails tucked neatly into black pencil-leg capris. Spiked springolators slapped against her heels as she paced from the living room to the bar area. She held her Viceroy cigarette at arm's length and whipped it through the air with an off-with-their heads manner. I felt like an unwelcome bug politely sipping my ginger ale while they downed cocktails in their spacious, modern living room. Loren patronizingly addressed me as "dear." She scrutinized my face with a forced smile.

"You look just like your mother, dear."

Then my father drunkenly blurted, "Your mother was the most beautiful woman I've ever seen in my life."

As that little gem fell from my father's lips, Loren lost her cool.

"Sheeee's the most beautiful? How dare you!" she shrieked. Loren flung her dry martini in my father's besotted face, and they wrestled to the floor. Whatever fantasies I had had over the past seven years of living with my dad were gone, out the window. After the scuffle Loren said that if my dad wanted me here so badly, we could sleep together in the guest bedroom. Loren stormed into the guestroom off the hall, and began making up the double bed in silent fury. As she shook out the pink top sheet it billowed with air and landed neatly on the mat-tress. Holy Mary, was I really going to have to sleep with my father to-night? At the last minute my dad, who was still drinking, thankfully said, "Come on, we're getting out of here."

Instead of the Corvette my dad was going to take the Cadillac in the garage. Loren chased after us and screamed, "You are not taking my car!"

She flung her body in front of the opened driver's side door, and the next thing I knew her fingers were smashed in the slamming door. She sadly held out her crushed, bleeding fingers, screaming, "And don't even think about coming back here with her!"

We ended up taking the Corvette and my tipsy dad sped down Mulholland as if the cops were chasing us. I was terrified as we slid around tight curves with the tires squealing. My dad, being a race-car driver, used only the high gears to slow us down, and I felt my body pressing hard against the passenger door from the speed and the force of the narrow corners.

"Forget about her," he slurred. "I have some nice friends in San Francisco, you wanna drive up there with me?"

At this point I wanted to be anywhere but in a race car with my dad, who was swigging Jack Daniel's straight from the bottle.

"I don't think I'd better," I squeaked.

He seemed a bit miffed, but after a hair-raising ride, I was thankfully back at Ozeta Terrace, and my dad disappeared back into the night.

My aunt Claire was already waiting at the front door.

"So how was it, how was seeing your father?"

I didn't bother to commiserate with her. The evening was really nothing out of the ordinary for my family; this was how they related to each other. It didn't really matter how anyone felt or was affected; I came from a family of self-centered egocentrics. Everyone else, includ-ing myself, was like a prop, a mirror to reflect his or her bad behavior.

"He was fine," I sighed, and left it at that.

Through her glory years my aunt Claire had amassed a plethora of sundries, extravagant costumes, and endless beautiful accessories. There were so many shoes and dresses that she had turned three entire bedrooms into walk-in closets. Two rooms were wall-to-wall clothes racks with aisles of silky gowns, furs, and extraordinary vintage dresses. Each piece was meticulously tagged and labeled from the 1930s to the present. Another room was floor-to-ceiling with barely worn shoes and period hats, mostly from Bullock's Wilshire, and all in their original vintage boxes. It was like the choicest wardrobe section at Hollywood's Western Costume. Through the mothball sachets you could still smell the powdery perfume and faded glamour. This wondrous old home was once full of life and dreams. Now it was only my old grandmother Helen with a touch of Alzheimer's, my fading aunt Claire and her son, Blake, marching aimlessly in his military attire.

I slept that night in the room with the clatter of the clocks, and to this day I can't sleep with a timepiece within earshot.

In the morning Claire drove me back in her 1949 classic black Cadillac. It was four blocks back to my mother's house.

"You're supposed to be living with your mother," she said. "Now go home."

*I*n the few months I'd been away, things had changed on Harriet Street. It was 1961, and Diana had fallen back in love; this time she had found herself a charismatic folk singer. He was part of a successful folk group of the early sixties. The group was flying high on several gold records, and was a sellout at all their venues, including the Hollywood Bowl.

He was handsome, tall and lanky with magnetic elegance and charm to spare. My mother actually seemed to soften under his melodic spell. He serenaded her with his original and Spanish love songs, and kept her days and nights occupied between the sheets. Diana was completely absorbed in her new traveling minstrel, and in short time our house turned into a happening folk hangout. Everyone from a young Leon Russell to Glen Campbell crossed our threshold. The big, burly Hoyt Axton wrote his hit song "Greenback Dollar" in our living room, and we even had a full-on bluegrass band, the Dillards, camp out in our house for over a month. Our two-story Craftsman house rang with amazing music and exotic drugs late into the dawn. I was relieved when we had company, as it averted Diana's tyrannical focus away from me.

Even though my bleak circumstances had slightly improved, Mitch Jayne, the bass fiddle player for the Dillards, was sufficiently concerned with the way my parents treated me to come up with a plan to rescue me. His wife and daughter lived in Missouri, and he was simply going to put me on a plane and send me to live with his family in secret. We were actually about to go through with the crazy plot. To introduce myself I wrote his wife a letter of gratitude and hid it under my mattress. The next day when I went to mail it, it had disappeared. My heart almost stopped on the spot. My mother found the letter and that was the end of that. The Dillards moved on.

We'd moved into the early sixties, and although we were comfortable enough, my mother still had very strange notions about nutrition. Basically, the food in our house was only for her, and she'd beat us to bruises if we dared to touch it. She had a refrigerator chock full with rotting morsels, but my brother Scot and I were not allowed to partake until the food became unrecognizable with mold and frothy decay. She hoarded perishables in her bedroom, and kept two special cupboards in the kitchen. One was her personal reserve, emblazoned with a wrathful sign warning my brother and me: "Keep your fucking hands out." The shelf for us was sparsely stocked with surplus canned food and an occasional package of Saltine crackers, and even then we had to ask permission to open a tin. Diana was, however, quite generous with the Tabasco sauce. She kept a foreboding bottle in plain view on the sill above the sink. She called the hot sauce "lie medicine." Whenever she suspected a falsehood or disrespect, my brother or I would have to serve ourselves a red-hot spoonful. If we were out of pepper sauce, a swig of dishwashing liquid would suffice. The same rule also applied to our dog, Tolly. Diana kept the wolfhound bound to a chair, with a footlong tether. The dog was as thin as a corpse and only got enough dry rations to keep her alive. She also wasn't allowed water because she'd pee in the house. I felt sorry seeing our dog suffer, and I'd secretly feed her when my mother was sleeping. For me, I basically survived on pinching Hershey bars from the candy display at Turner's liquor store on Sunset.

You'd never know by looking at the folk singer's handsome face, but his dark side surpassed even my mother's. He preferred psychological to physical abuse. His crazy tortures were far more sophisticated and carefully thought out. One night he sat me down and made me stare close into his eyes without looking away. After the first half hour his face would appear to contort and morph into scary-looking demons. With his eyes locked and piercing deeply into mine, he'd say chilling things to me: "I have the power to take you to places you've never imagined; I can show you the deepest depths, the darkest corners of hell." And I believed him. He had several sadistic rituals that came from out of the blue. Sometimes he'd have me or my brother lean against a wall, bearing all our weight on one finger until it ached like fire, or he'd have me stand on one leg till it got so tired I'd fall to the floor.

One night he told me, "Get in the car, we're going for a ride."

It was rare that I went anywhere with the dark duo, and wondered, where could we be going? We drove way past Hollywood, deep into the barrio. When we got to the dilapidated depths of downtown Los Angeles and hit the railroad yard, he stopped the car and my mother simply told me to get out. They then drove off, leaving me on a dark and desolate road next to the train tracks. There was no one around but a few drunken bums teetering in the distance, and I was terrified. It wasn't just that my parents had left me there; I was just a little girl, only eleven years old and completely vulnerable to the perilous elements.

Down the road I saw a cluster of friendly bushes, a small bit of sanctuary to hide myself in. I didn't know what to do except stay out of sight and wait for the sun to rise. I worried that the local drunken derelicts would spot me and maybe kidnap me, or worse. Hours later I saw Diana and her folk singer circling the block, and I ran from the brush waving my arms. I don't know why they came back for me. Maybe they hoped I'd just disappear but then thought better of it. Maybe it was their twisted way of showing me the grim alternative, and how grateful I should be that they were kind enough to let me live in their house.

We got back to Harriet Street around midnight and the folk singer brought out the Bible. He turned to the Book of Ruth and instructed me to read it, and then to write a thesis on Ruth's life. When that was finished I was to write a paper about my loving, devoted family, about how fortunate I was to have one. Before they went off to bed my mother gave me one of her Dexamil uppers, and watched to make sure I swallowed it.

The Book of Ruth was a story of obedience, piety, and sacrifice. It wasn't an easy read. I also had to keep in mind the spin of what they wanted me to write. By the time I finished Ruth and the two essays it was already dawn. I still felt flibberty from the Dexamil, but it was time to get ready for school.

West Hollywood Elementary was my refuge, a brief repose from my secret life at home. This month my class was studying drug awareness, with a spotlight on marijuana, the dangers of wacky weed. I'm sure I was the only one in my sixth-grade class with firsthand information. At my house you could get high just walking through the front door.

I wanted to join the school orchestra, and had my heart set on the cello. When I asked my mother if she would sign the paper authorizing me to take the instrument home for practice, I got a plain and simple no.

"The cello is not for you."

She couldn't bear for me to have anything of my own. Even when my grandmother Mimi sent me a birthday gift, Diana returned it to the store and exchanged it for something for herself. She said Mimi was her mother, not mine.

Diana never missed a day without reproaching me. She said I was unsightly, and constantly criticized me: "Why couldn't you have been more like me?"

Even the sound of my breath sent her into a rage. I became so self-conscious, I could barely move without first contemplating it. I didn't understand her fury toward me. All I knew was that I was powerless to change it. I don't think it was my unfolding beauty, as I'd been a source of irritation since I was born. I just became accustomed to her madness.

There was a stunning pivotal moment when my mother was screaming and trying to beat the life out of me because I'd misplaced one of her sewing needles. She woke me in the middle of the night, and I couldn't find it. I remember thinking, maybe she was right, maybe I was round the bend and bad to the bone. I just didn't know it because I was crazy. For a moment I thought if I just gave in and accepted that I was not sane, things might be better between us. I was about to acquiesce, to jump off the deep, when I heard a loud clear voice in my head echoing, "*No!*"

My mother had taken every possible thing away from me—except me. As hard as she tried, as evil as she was, she couldn't manage to crush my spirit. The one attractive thing I knew I possessed was a soft mane of long blond hair. Strangely, it hadn't occurred to her before. I must have turned my head in a certain light that got her attention. She said to the folk singer, "Let's cut her hair off."

For me, my hair was like a protective veil in which I could conceal any and all emotions; I felt almost invisible with just a tilt of my head. With her long, pointy sewing shears, my mother roughly chopped off my locks in short clumps above my ears, leaving fresh jagged scissor cuts across the nape of my neck. She tossed the long strands on the carpet while her boyfriend merely looked on.

"That's better," she said. "Now, you look your age."

In the morning, no matter how I brushed, wet, teased, or tucked it I looked as if I'd been skinned. As a last-ditch effort, I covered my freshly cropped head with a dark blue kerchief and plodded off to West Hollywood Elementary School. I don't know which was more odd, coming into my classroom sporting a scarf or the state of my new 'do. The teacher told me the head covering was inappropriate in class and insisted I remove it. After the unveiling there was a clamor in the classroom, as if I'd arrived half undressed; the teacher quickly softened and told me I could keep my head covered up for the day.

I lived in a constant state of terror. When school let out adrenaline pumped through my heart because I knew I had to go home. What would happen today? Would I be tortured, pounded, or simply shunned? If I was lucky, Diana and the folk singer would still be asleep. I assumed that parents hated their children, and wondered why they ever had them. When I went to bed at night I'd pray not to wake up. When my mother went out I'd pray, "Please don't let her come home tonight."

When she slept extra late, I was hopeful: Maybe she was dead.

I came home from school one afternoon to find my four-year-old brother Scot buck naked and doing his best to hold back his big salty tears. Since he'd gotten a bit older, he'd joined the rank of "enemy" status and wasn't treated much better than myself. Scot was in the middle of our living room wearing only his little cowboy boots, trying to stay balanced on one leg. All his playthings and clothes were heaped in the garbage bin because he didn't deserve them anymore. I knew the drill; it was one of the folk singer's maniacal Nazi rituals. If my brother's leg got tired and touched the floor before the fifteen minutes were up, Scot would have to start his time all over again with the other leg. All of this was because my brother had forgotten to take the dog out while I was in school, and the pup had pooped on the carpet.

I felt helpless, and knew I was unable to do anything to stop the crazy abuse. As hard as I prayed, they wouldn't go away. I knew I wouldn't survive living with the folk singer and Diana until I reached eighteen, when I could legally leave home. I went to my room, closed the door, and slipped out the window with nothing but the clothes I was wearing. I never saw that house or was subjected to either of them again. Unfortunately my little brother didn't fare as well. He later told me horror stories of our mother giving him LSD when he was just six years old. She wanted to see his reaction, and tape-recorded his whole ungodly trip. Eventually his grandparents on Uncle Daddy's side stepped in and took Scot to live under their protective wings.

At eleven years old I didn't really have anywhere to go. Mimi and Al were vacationing at the Eden Roc in Florida, and my dad and his nutty wife, Loren, were not an option. I wandered the Sunset Strip, and when the sun went down I took refuge in a vacant utility room in an underground parking lot on the Strip. I made myself comfortable on a mound of stacked cardboard boxes and spent the night in pitch-blackness.

That night I had the most stunning dream.

I walked into a grand old theater with ornate architecture and celestial murals. There were long purple velvet curtains covering a passageway. When I went to peek through the drapes, I fell fast into a deep dark shaft. I tried to grasp the walls to slow myself down, but I just tumbled faster. I thought I was going to die, but then I saw a faint light at the end of the tunnel, which got blindingly brighter. When I reached the light I was dropped into an ocean with no land in sight. The water was warm and gently enveloping, and the sun reflected off the ripples, creating infinite glistening stars. Even though I was in the middle of a deep blue sea I felt no fear, only all-encompassing love.

There was no actual voice, but something spoke inside: "Do you know where you are?"

Without words I answered, "Yes, I'm with God."

Then I serenely floated off into eternal bliss.

For the first time that I could remember, I woke up feeling peaceful, but also starving. I walked across the street to Turner's liquor store and stole my usual breakfast, a Hershey's bar with almonds. I then drifted over to West Hollywood Park on San Vicente. Sitting at the top of the bleachers, finishing off the last bit of chocolate, I felt happy. I was free, but to do what? I couldn't go back to school, and I really had nowhere to go, but I knew the good Lord always provides. Later that night I was arrested in front of Ben Frank's Coffee Shop on Sunset, and landed safely at the West Hollywood sheriff's station. All the police wanted to do was take me back home. I told the officers my name was Mary, and refused to disclose any more personal information. I felt sure that if I breathed a word of what went on in my house, the cops wouldn't believe me, or worse, they'd call my parents and I'd be done for. The sheriffs tried to frighten me by telling one the woes of reformatory lockup.

"Believe us, once you get there you'll wish you were back home."

"No I won't," I peeped. "I want to go there."

When I wouldn't budge about who I was or where I lived, a squad car with a caged-in backseat arrived, and drove me to my next destination, Los Padrinos, a state institution for delinquents in downtown Downey.

Los Padrinos was slightly scarier than I'd imagined. It was basically a teen prison full of harder fish than myself. There were actual steel bars on the doors that opened with electronic buzzers. I soon realized I was in jail. It was after midnight when I arrived, and I was taken to an echoing shower room and given a brown paper bag to put my personal effects in. After the spa treatment they checked me for bugs and any other contraband. Once I passed the inspection I was issued a bundle of standard prison fare. The package contained one stiff cotton nightdress and an oversized frock that looked as if it had been pressed in an old-fashioned mangle. The king-sized panties were big enough for three of me; I had to knot them at my waist to keep them from falling down around my ankles. The wardress led me down a bleak sterile hall while her jangle of keys slapped against her butt, alerting the other inmates that fresh blood had arrived. She deposited me in unit L and locked the door securely behind her.

My tiny barren cell was lima bean green with a steely bed bolted to the cement floor. There was a toilet with no seat, a small sink, and a mirror riveted to the wall, and that was about it. Even the windows were covered in metal mesh for additional security. My dense steel door had a small window to look out into the hallway or, more likely, for the guards to peer in. The only thing that really concerned me was that they never turned the lights completely out. My little spot on the planet was in perpetual twilight.

I made up my bunk with the state-issued stiff sheets and smoothed out my gray wool blanket. Lying in bed I noticed the profusion of etched and written graffiti from the previous inmates. It covered the walls like decorative paper. There were names like "Lil Dot" and "Angel Por Vida." It was even on the ceiling. I wondered how they managed to carve it all the way up there. It was late in the night and unit L was as quiet as a church. I felt tears streaming down the sides of my face, but they were tears of relief. Maybe I was a little scared, but I'd saved myself, I felt safe. The real nightmare was over.

The morning was a bit of a shock. I was roused from slumber at 5:00 A.M. with an onset of buzzers and clanking metal doors. I quickly dressed in my stiff, starched reformatory frock, which hung on my thin frame like rigid cardboard. The unit doors were opened, and each girl stood at attention in front of her respective coop. The chattering

inmates passed a metal bucket of disinfectant water down the hall. After we swabbed and sterilized our concrete cells we all lined up for
breakfast. I noticed I was the youngest and the only Caucasian lass on
the block. My partners in residence were divided into elite little
cliques, the Bloods, the Compton girls, and a small crew of Chicanas.
Where were all the girls from Hollywood? I was clearly out of my inexperienced league.

There wasn't much of an academic program, mainly a few unin-
spiring craft classes. Outside volunteers came in and taught us how to
crochet poodle-head hair spray cozies or glue Popsicle sticks into picture frames. Once a day we were allowed out into the barbed-wired
compound for a bit of sunshine and exercise. We couldn't just loll
around on our own, though, we had to be in a single-file march. We
did it military style while shouting a rousing little jingle: "I don't know
but I've been told, unit L is mighty bold." "Sound off, say it again."
That's the only bit of the verse I remember, but the girls also dragged
one leg like it was stiff or broken to the beat. On Fridays we had talent
night in the gymnasium, where the female inmates danced together,
and lip-synced to Motown records. I learned how to do an authentic
"Harlem Shuffle," and dance the "Hitch Hike" to Marvin Gaye.

The most inspiring part of my Los Padrinos experience was Miss
Moon's gospel choir. Miss Moon was a spirited little black woman who
sang with her soul, and loved teaching delinquent girls the gospel. Of
course I joined on the spot, and looked forward to Sunday services. I
loved dressing in the shimmery satin choir gown and singing up on the
church stage. We'd start off with a soulful "Bringing in the Sheaves,"
then bring the house down with a revival of "Rock My Soul in the Bo-
som of Abraham," our hands shaking in the air "praise Jesus" style:
"Oh-rocka-ma-soul."

Two uneventful months passed. I had therapists, administrators,
and concerned social workers all coming to talk with me, trying to de-

code the "mystery girl." No matter how they cajoled and prodded, I wasn't giving out any information. I thought I was actually getting away with the ruse, but then came the voice of doom. I was busy putting the finishing pom-poms on a hair spray cozy when a monitor popped in and announced that I had visitors. The jolt of adrenaline just about knocked me over. Sure enough, it was the wicked witch and her evil sidekick Beelzebub, disguised as kindly mortals.

While the social worker stood by, my well-dressed mother and her dashing minstrel were as cordial as Ozzie and Harriet. As soon we got into the private visiting room my mother slapped me so hard it left a hot-pink hand print across my cheek.

"I hope you're happy, because I've made you a ward of the court," she snarled. "You will rot here until you turn eighteen."

I suppose she thought that would be upsetting to me, but I couldn't have been more happy. I don't think it even occurred to her, but in signing me over to the state she forever lost her power over me. I was legally safe now. Seven years in detention did sound like eternity, but it was certainly preferable to going back to Hades on Harriet Street. I had prevailed.

Soon after their visit I received a fresh white envelope from Florida with the Eden Roc Hotel emblem. It was a comforting letter from my grandmother Mimi telling me she was on her way to the rescue. Mimi said springing me from the system wasn't going to be easy. My mother had refused to sign papers releasing me to her, and adoption was out of the question. My grandparents took her to court, and it dragged on for a year, finally ending with a compromise and an exchange of cash. I wasn't allowed to live with Mimi and Al, but I could be moved to a privately funded institution and have overnight weekend visitation with them.

The one constant thing in my life, the thing that kept me sound, was my belief in God, my recurring dreams of Jesus, and my affinity for Catholicism. It was my shield, my sacred sway. Even when I lived with my mother and the folk singer I'd risk their rage and sneak off to the neighborhood church on Sundays. While they were still sleeping I'd take my little brother, Scot, to the Sunday school, then go upstairs to the comforting mass. My religious belief could not be shaken, but I was about to face a new, opposing doctrine.

Vista del Mar was a low-security Jewish orphanage, and also a home for children awaiting placement or unable to live in their own homes. The English translation meant "View of the Sea." I couldn't see the ocean, but the orphanage was a charming, self-contained, coed compound that was built on a ranch in West Los Angeles in 1925 for Jewish orphans. It had well-kept grounds, tennis courts, and an Olympic-sized swimming pool. It also had an infirmary and its own imposing temple for worship. There were five two-story cottages that housed twenty children each, all set back on a lush, tree-lined lane. It looked like the back lot of a movie studio and was sometimes used as a film location. In order to be placed there, you were supposed to be of the Jewish faith. The only reason I'd been admitted was that my grandfather was a member of the prestigious Friars Club and had been a substantial benefactor over the years. It was the nicest and least re-stricted place they could get me into. In order to live there I would be expected to learn Hebrew, attend all religious services, and uphold Or-thodox high holidays.

After my stint in Los Padrinos and sovereignty from my crazy mother, I'd turned into a bit of a rebel. At twelve I'd already had more life experience than most of the adults in charge. I had a nothing-to-lose attitude, and little interest in learning the philosophy of Judaism. I was still the girl who wanted to become a nun. I was aware that my religious views were less than popular, and airing them in Hebrew class caused me to forgo a few weekend visits with my grandparents, but I couldn't help myself. I never missed an opportunity to exasperate poor old Mr. Solomon with my contrary Catholic scripture and religious rhetoric. I was no Judas. To the teacher's credit, I did learn to read, write, and speak the language. I even learned to say the Sabbath blessing in Hebrew. Except for the religious classes we were bused to a public school, Palms Junior High in posh Cheviot Hills.

It didn't take long to realize that the kids from the home were not at the top of the popularity pole. We were a sort of oddity because we didn't live with our own families, and there were other subtle differences that set us apart. During Passover we weren't allowed to eat leavened bread. When we showed up at the lunch quad with peanut butter and matzoh sandwiches we might as well have been Martians. I was the real alien. I didn't feel any more at home with this flock than I did with the gang girls at Los Padrinos.

I lived for Fridays, when Mimi picked me up for the weekend and scurried me off to her home in Beverly Hills.

She took me swimming at the fashionable Racket Club, and shopping in Beverly Hills, and we'd have early dinner at the Hamburger Hamlet before going back to my home away from home. Mimi always promised, "We're working on it, love, it won't be long, soon we'll have you home for good."

My life was a grab bag; I never knew what was going to happen next. There was no foundation or continuity; everything was subject to change. No direction or dreams were allowed. I just drifted from place to place as an onlooker in everyone else's extraordinary play. I had no concept of trust. In the eyes of the orphanage I was a willful rebel, but my focus was only to survive with my spirit intact.

With a chance encounter, my life was about to change. My old friend Richard, the one who two years earlier had professed his crazy love for me, had been keeping an eye on my state of affairs. He even wrote letters to the court on my behalf, trying to get me released from Los Padrinos. While I was stuck in the pokey Mimi and Richard had become fast friends. Mimi didn't have a clue about Richard's obsession with her young granddaughter; she just thought he was a concerned ally. They shared stories about Diana's mistreatment of me, and worked on ideas of how to get me free. Even though Richard was something of a pedophile, a condition I didn't know existed, he'd also been one of the few sources of support in my young life. Besides taking me to the doctor to get my broken arm patched, he seemed to have genuine concern for me. I wasn't into the love vibe, but I still liked Richard as long as he wasn't trying to get my pants off.

When I got settled into Vista del Mar we exchanged some innocent letters, and I spoke with him from the payphone on the grounds. Richard, being a club owner, knew all the up-and-coming talents. He also had an acquaintance with the relatively unknown twenty-two-year-old folksinger Bob Dylan. Bob was in Los Angeles from Woodstock to play a concert in Santa Monica, and Richard asked if I'd like to go along. Luckily it was the weekend with my grandparents, and Richard convinced Mimi that seeing Bob Dylan in concert would be most educational. She was skeptical but let me go to the Saturday night show.

The mysterious, lanky Bob Dylan shuffled out onto the stage and mesmerized my fertile mind with "The Times They Are A-Changin'," "Blowin' in the Wind," and the "Girl from the North Country."

Bob Dylan was the most beautiful man I'd ever seen. His soft curls were longer than regulation, and his skin was smooth and pale, with just a hint of a beard.

After the show we went backstage, and Bob introduced himself, holding out his long expressive hand to greet me. He had a gentle quality with a nervous edge. When I looked into his hazel green eyes I felt a new peculiar shiver, like a quiver of lightning hitting my heart.

There was a party at the home of Bob's booking agent, Ben Shapiro, in the Hollywood Hills, and Bob asked if I would like to go with him.

Richard said I could go, and that he'd meet us there. I didn't know it at the time, but Richard had filled him in on my weary background, so Bob took me under his wing. The party was at the top of King's Road, above Sunset, at a rambling old Spanish-style home. The smoldering *Sketches of Spain* by Miles Davis echoed throughout the amber candle-lit rooms that were full of art, antiques, and grainy photographs of blues and folk heroes. The floors were hardwood with Oriental rugs and big pillows to sit on. It was all wonderfully bohemian.

Bob and I talked for hours in front of the glowing fireplace. He was impervious to the looming, amorous folk chicks and record executives who wanted their moment with him. We talked about forgiveness, which was something I'd never even thought about, or believed I could accomplish. He told me about strength of spirit, which I knew I possessed, and the freedom of having nothing to lose. He was so right. I'd never had anything to lose. At the end of the night Bob wrote his phone number and address in Woodstock on a little piece of paper and told me I could call him collect.

I bought Bob's first album and played it till the grooves wore thin. My unenlightened fellow inmates at the orphanage did not share my enthusiasm. It was 1963, I was thirteen years old, and the Beatles had just arrived on the scene with "She Loves You." They actually scorned Bob's music and hated his voice. They all laughed at me when I played his album. I defended Bob.

"You'll see, one day he's going to be a famous poet."

I was in love with the sweet gruff sound of "Corrina Corrina," "Pretty Peggy-O," and "Baby, Let Me Follow You Down." I wondered who Rick Von Schmidt was, and dreamed of going to Greenwich Village. Mimi bought me a guitar, and I taught myself the chords to "Don't Think Twice, It's All Right" and "Blowin' in the Wind." My head was full of Bob Dylan's words, and of running away to New York City.

The next time Bob came to town he picked me up outside the gate of the orphanage. He was waiting in a white Mustang convertible. Bob didn't drive, but he had his friend Victor Maymudes behind the wheel, and we took the backseat. Of course, I didn't have permission to leave the grounds, but barbed razor wire wouldn't have stopped me.

Victor drove us to the beach, dropping us off at the Santa Monica pier. We played games on the boardwalk, and Bob popped enough balloons at the dart gallery to win me a furry stuffed Tweety Bird. There was a funky little beach café next to the merry-go-round. We fed a couple of quarters into the jukebox and took a seat in the corner. Bob played "She Loves You" and "I Want to Hold Your Hand" by the new group, the Beatles. He said he liked their chord changes, and played them a few times in a row. Sipping my root beer to the Fab Four, and talking with Bob Dylan. I couldn't have been in better company. We discussed my precarious situation. I described how I ended up in the institution and my malevolence toward my mother. Bob said I wouldn't be able to see it now, but one day she'd be friendless and alone. I tried hard to imagine his words, but I couldn't picture my almighty, invincible mother deflated and without an audience. He said this was my life, my gift, that I had choices and didn't need to follow anyone's rules. "It's only life," he said.

For a thirteen-year-old it was a bit cryptic, but I understood the essence. I was free.

It was dusk when we got back to the orphanage, and we drove right onto the grounds in the Mustang. Besides the Beatles, I don't think any of my cohorts at Vista del Mar had ever seen anyone with long hair, and Bob was causing a bit of a stir. Some of the kids gathered around the convertible, jeering, "Is it a boy or is it a girl?" I was mortally embarrassed, and later promised the infidels, "One day you're going to remember this, and you'll all be sorry."

I knew that by bringing Bob and Victor onto the property, I'd forfeited my weekend visit with my grandparents, and would be restricted to my room for the next month. I didn't care. It was well worth the price of admission.

Another time I slipped out and went with Bob to visit the revolutionary comic Lenny Bruce. I remembered my mother used to go to see his shows at the Unicorn, but I had little idea that I was in the presence of another legend. Lenny lived at the top of a hill above Sunset. His home wasn't stately or flash. It was a simple sixties stucco structure with modern decor and a large picture window that overlooked the Sunset Strip. Bob and I only spent a few hours at his home, but I remember Lenny as looking damp and behaving somewhat frantically. He had a high-powered telescope poised at the window, aimed at the famed Schwab's pharmacy. I remember Bob playing Lenny a few of his new songs, and Lenny spending most of the time spying on unsuspecting pedestrians in front of the drugstore.

When Bob went back to Woodstock I wrote him lengthy girlish letters and called him collect for more words of enlightenment and wisdom. There were never any romantic overtones, at least on his part. I believe he favored me because of my extraordinary history and situation. In 1963 it was still uncommon to hear about child abuse and abandonment. Kids weren't taking drugs or running away. It was a more gentle time. I also think he liked my innocent enthusiasm and the fact that I got it. I understood what he was saying.

By age fourteen I'd begun to blossom into my slender frame. I had loose blond locks and lofty ideas. I started sneaking out of the dormitory at night and taking the bus—from Venice to West Hollywood. With my guitar in tow, I'd head straight for the Troubadour. The Troubadour was a hot little folk club on Santa Monica Boulevard that dripped with intrigue and a new kind of music. It was a rustic little hole-in-the-wall with theater seats in the back and parlor tables right up to the stage. It was a place where all of the up-to-the-minute folk heroes came to play music and hang out, where pretty young waitresses served apple cider with cinnamon sticks. I finally had a budding direction, a dream of my own. I wanted to be a writer, a poet, to sing and play music.

I wasn't really old enough to be hanging out at the Troubadour, but because it was known that my stepfather was a famous folk singer, I got special treatment. Mondays were Hoot Nights, when anyone could get up and perform. You could usually find Jim, a.k.a. Roger McGuinn, in the dark adjoining lounge doing his version of Beatles songs, and cherub-faced David Crosby performing with his band, the Balladeers. I also had a giant teen crush on young Crosby, which helped to motivate my weekly escape from the institution. David would sometimes accompany me on guitar, and sweetly flirted, saying, "Ah, if you were just five years older." I made a splash singing "The Times They Are A-Changin'" and "Don't Think Twice, It's All Right." One night a music scout from Liberty Records approached me, but I had to decline, as I wasn't supposed to be there in the first place.

One Friday night Mimi picked me up with a bit of bad news. The courts had ruled against us. I wouldn't be allowed to live with her or anyone else. My rambling religious debates, rendezvous with Bob Dylan, and late-night excursions to the Troubadour hadn't helped my position either. Because I hadn't gone along with the program at the orphanage, the chances were good I'd be going back to Los Padrinos until I turned eighteen, or maybe even twenty-one. I had a sick feeling in my stomach, like trying to avoid an imminent car crash. I couldn't stand another four years of being locked up. I thought about what Bob had said: "It's your life."

On Sunday night Mimi drove me back to Vista del Mar, promising she'd figure something out. She pleaded, "Love, please try to get along here."

"Okay, Mimi, I will."

I kissed her soft powdery cheek good-bye, told her I loved her, then bounded up the stairs to my dormitory to pack for the road. I stuffed a Mexican straw bag with a faded pair of Levi's, the loose olive green pullover Mimi had knitted for me, my handmade leather beatnik sandals, and most important my *Freewheelin'* Bob Dylan album. I grabbed one last thing: a full bottle of Bayer aspirin. I'd heard that swallowing a whole jar was as lethal as heart failure. If I got caught, I'd kill myself.

It was dark when I slipped out the back door. I didn't have a clue how I was going to get there, but I was on my way to Greenwich Village, New York City. My real adventure was about to begin.

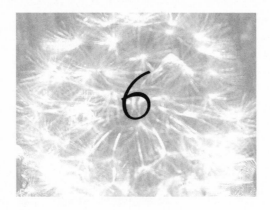

6

With a sense of terror and excitement, and without a penny in my pocket, I was on my way. I hoofed it for two long hours, and eventually reached my first stop. Where else? The Troubadour. Holy Mary, my poor heart! The cops were already on my trail. When I walked through the door I saw two police officers passing my school picture around in the adjacent lounge. I wondered how they had found me so fast. Fortunately, the club was packed to the rafters, and I was able to squeeze past the crowd and into the darkness of the showroom. Ramblin' Jack Elliott was taking his final bow when I spotted the only vacant seat in the back row. As my belly leaped with adrenaline, I slid down low and whispered to the unknowing stranger in the seat next to me, "Pretend like you know me."

He slid his arm around my shoulder as if we were a couple, and over Ramblin' Jack's applause and accolades I whispered again, "The police are chasing me; can you help me get out of here?"

The stranger motioned that he was parked in the back, and when the audience cheered for a last encore, we casually slipped out of the rear exit. With no concern at all I jumped into the car and put my head down out of sight. My gallant savior covered me with his coat, and we sped away into the night. Once we were on the Hollywood Freeway he relaxed.

"It's all clear, you can sit up now."

I popped out from under his coat and got a closer look at my emancipator.

Michael Stewart was a lanky young man in his early twenties. He had longish brown, wispy hair, huge blue eyes, and a gentle, almost modest demeanor. I told him of my wild state of affairs, and he was eager to help. He said he had some art student friends who lived in the mountains near Claremont; perhaps I could hide out there.

After an hour of winding country roads, we arrived at an old, secluded clapboard house nestled high in the hills, surrounded by grand old pines and lush-smelling firs. The air had a crisp chill and the moon was full with a smile. I leaped up the fifty steep steps to the front door, where I met Frank and Will.

Michael introduced me as his fourteen-year-old runaway.

"Can she hide out here for a few days?"

Will, exhaling a cloud of pot smoke, said, "Yeah, that's cool; she can sleep in the spare room."

The spare room had the feeling of an abandoned house, furnished with just a lumpy old iron bed and yellowed pull-down shades. Later that night I stared out at the stars and listened to the comforting chorus of crickets. I wasn't the least bit afraid. I said my prayers, thanking God, and fell asleep thinking, "Wow, I really did it."

Michael showed up the next day to check on his ward, and treated me to a hamburger at the local diner. It turned out he was a guitar player and had his own little group called We Five. Each night he'd pick me up for a bit of dinner and I'd tag along to his band practice.

Rehearsals were held at the singer Beverly's parents' house just a few miles away. I must have heard "You Were On My Mind" a hundred times and never got tired of it.

Michael had some encouraging news for me. He'd spoken with his brother, who was in the market for a nanny; if it worked out, I might be going to live in San Francisco.

His brother was John Stewart, lead singer of the Kingston Trio. He lived up north in Mill Valley with his wife and two blond toddlers, but the Trio was in Los Angeles recording a new album at Capitol. Michael picked me up and drove me to the album-shaped Capitol Records recording studio on Franklin and Vine. The next thing I knew I was on a flight to San Francisco.

I never did see Michael again, but often thought about how differently things might have turned out. What if someone else had been sitting next to that empty seat at the Troubadour?

Mill Valley was a quiet little artsy community just across the Golden Gate Bridge from San Francisco. I had really lucked out. John's wife treated me like her own daughter. She decorated a room for me, took me shopping for stylish new clothes, and bought me my first pair of pumps with petite high heels. I was paid ten dollars a week to help with chores and look after their children. It felt so legitimate. I'd become part of a real family, but deep down I knew it couldn't last, it couldn't be that easy. I felt like Richard Kimble, the TV fugitive, always expecting a tap on the shoulder or a platoon of cops to nab me off the street and send me back to Hollywood.

I'd been happily living with the Stewarts for three months when John thought it would be a good idea to enroll me in the local junior high school. That was my cue to scram. He said we would get a good attorney, maybe they would even adopt me. I knew that could never happen. He had never come up against anyone like my mother, and didn't have a clue of what she was capable of. There was no doubt she'd rather see me locked away than living with a nice family. I envisioned myself back in steely handcuffs, back in the dispirited, medicinal halls of Los Padrinos. The Stewarts tried to reassure me, but I couldn't chance it. I left a letter of gratitude, then headed back on course, toward my original destination: New York City.

I met some hippie kids at Sausalito Park and hitched a ride with them over the Oakland Bay Bridge to Berkeley. Our target was the renowned Telegraph Avenue.

It was 1964, the early days of peace, love, and psychedelic euphoria, the onset of the teenage revolution. The street had a magical atmosphere, alive with a kaleidoscope of colorfully dressed minstrels, beggars, poets, pretty young girls, and handsome boys with mutinous long hair. Enchanting fragrances of frankincense, patchouli, and burning hashish permeated the air like a mysterious mist. I'd never seen anything like this in Hollywood.

I met a boy on Telegraph Avenue who was wearing the coolest pair of sunglasses. They were vintage with tan Lucite frames, and forest green lenses. I commented, "Great shades."

He peered out over the top of them. "I bet they'd look better on you," he said, then placed them over my eyes.

"Do you live around here?"

"No, I just got here. I don't have a place to stay yet."

"Don't worry," he beamed. "I'll look after you."

Nicky had the most soulful, resplendent hazel-green eyes and a boyish, infectious smile. His tousled brown hair just brushed the shoulders of his vintage suede jacket, and his stature was artistically slender. He walked with a cool, easy swagger, like a boy trying to be a man. He wrote poetry, chain-smoked, drove an old red Chevy pickup, and rocked on the guitar. Nicky had the spirit of a rebel, but possessed a young hero's heart; he was just fifteen.

His parents were blues singer Barbara Dane and guitar master Rolf

Cahn. They'd been divorced since he was a kid, and he'd been kicking around the city on his own, playing folk clubs since he was twelve. Not only had I found a like spirit, Nicky would be indirectly responsible for seeing me safely to New York.

As promised, he found me a place to stay with some political science students near the Berkeley campus. At night he'd pick me up in the Chevy truck and we made the rounds to all the local music scenes, then home to Telegraph Avenue for some late-night blues. We were a pair of adolescent kids, the runaway and the rebel, just living in the moment.

Nicky wrote me an extraordinary piece of blues that he'd composed on the guitar, called "Train Song." There was something about the simplicity, the nomadic, sad sound, like a train departing with hopeful dreams, taking you on life's journey, that always made me laugh. The gentle refrain would reduce me to tears, but by the end of the melody I'd be laughing again. "Train Song" had the unsatisfied tones of sweet sorrow, and youthful reverie. When he played it I could envision my life unfolding, tripping, recklessly dancing, crashing toward my shaky destination. I could never get enough of the impassioned refrain. Even today, it still sends me.

One late night Nicky screeched up to the sorority house where I was staying and shouted up, "Hurry up, get in the truck, the cops are on the way!"

I had been in Berkeley for only a few weeks, but someone said there was an all points bulletin out on me. It seemed someone had squealed. I'd heard the police were fast on my trail, and had been showing my picture around the coffeehouses on Telegraph Avenue.

Nicky was taking me to his father's house two hours north in a small rural town called Inverness.

"No one will find you way out here," he assured me.

Inverness was a picturesque pastureland dotted with aging farmhouses, and with a quaint river running through the middle of town.

Nicky's dad, Rolf, looked like a bohemian Johnny Cash, all dressed in black with a handsome mane of raven hair and wise dark eyes. He gave his rebel son the suspicious eyebrow but graciously invited us to stay.

Up until now sexual intimacy hadn't been on the program, but this night would be something special. I made myself comfortable on Nicky's childhood bed as he serenaded me on his guitar. I knew what was about to happen, and it would be perfect.

We made passionate, ethereal love for hours in the dark. Kissing him was like tasting cool water in a parched desert. It felt like the room and everything in it had faded away. It was just us and the universe. The innocent passion between us was like a religious revival when the music reaches a fervor, releasing your spirit to the heavens. In the morning I watched as Nicky pulled on his Levi's with a crisp swoosh. The sexy jangle of his loose belt buckle, the sight of his smooth boyish chest made me feel almost faint. I wanted to climb inside, pass through him, be a part of him.

Nicky hadn't mentioned this to me earlier, but before we met he'd been living with an older woman of twenty-two, an airline hostess, who was back in Berkeley. He said he was going to break the news and tell her that it was over. He kissed me hard with his sweet teenage breath. "I'll be back soon, you'll be safe here." And he was gone.

The next day Rolf was busy packing his bags. He told me he was off to New York for a spell, but that I was welcome to stay. I couldn't believe he'd just leave me in this big old house in the middle of nowhere. There wasn't even a telephone.

I spent the week exploring the countryside, composing love sonnets and wondering when my sweet Nicky would return. Late in the afternoon I heard a light tap at the door. Instead of my young beau, there stood a jovial stout chap who said he'd come all the way from Boston just to visit with Rolf.

Arnold Cummins looked like an eccentric Kris Kringle, with his curly gray locks and toting a quaint black physician's bag. He was the original mild-mannered small-town doctor, the sort who still made house calls. He dabbled on guitar, had a passion for the blues, and was a giant fan of Rolf's music. Happy for a bit of company, I invited him in and we chatted the night away. I dazzled him with my youthful prose, knowledge of gospel music, and the story of how I came to be in Inverness. I was so busy nattering away that I hadn't noticed he'd fallen fast asleep. He was fully standing up but leaning on the door jam. It was the bearlike snore that gave him away. Arnold was the only person I'd ever known who could be dead asleep and still on his feet.

In the morning, as he was putting his suitcase in the car for his flight home, he paused.

"How would you like to come back to Boston and live with my family?"

I wondered about Nicky. He'd been gone for over a week—was he really coming back?

The next thing I knew I was on a jet plane heading east.

Arnold lived with his pretty wife, Sally, and their two young boys in the ritzy suburbs of Watertown, Massachusetts.

Boston had just had an early snow, and their Tudor manor looked like an old-fashioned Christmas card. Besides Arnold's family practice, the doctor also owned a hopping little coffeehouse in the city called the Turk's Head where the local talent performed. Arnold gave me a job in the lounge serving hot cider and cappuccinos, so I'd have a little pocket money. Once again I'd landed softly on my feet. The angels were with me, but my head and willful spirit were still full of Greenwich Village and seeing Bob Dylan again.

I'd been with the Cummins family for three weeks when sweet Doctor Arnold, who believed in dreams, confided that he had a friend who was driving down to New York on the weekend. He said if I still wanted to, I could go along for the drive. He gave me an extra twenty dollars to catch the Greyhound back to Boston, and I was on my way.

My ride stopped at the corner of Bleecker and MacDougal, right smack in the heart of the village.

"Is this okay?" he asked.

There were the Gaslight Cafe, the Blue Angel, Cafe Wha?, all the places I'd heard so much about.

"Yep, I think this is it."

I'd had a dream and a vision, an unwavering focus, and nothing had stopped me. It was as if a band of angels had spread their wings, spanning a gentle bridge for me to cross. I made it to New York City on the wings of angels.

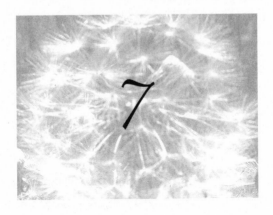

7

I tried to call Bob in Woodstock, but a female voice answered saying he had just gone on tour. Hmm, what next? I was so naïve I hadn't really thought of the small details, like where I was going to spend the night. The sun was beginning to set, and for the first time since the beginning of my journey, I was actually feeling frightened. Here I was, completely alone on the streets of a big city where I didn't know a soul. I wandered into Washington Square Park, where I heard music in the distance. It was one of those magical New York Indian summer evenings, and all these interesting-looking people were stirring around the village fountain like a swarm of fireflies. There were jugglers, holy rollers, artists, lone guitarists, and small gatherings of people playing music. The amusing thing was, most of the boys sounded and appeared just like junior Bob Dylans. They all wore their little Dylan caps with Hohner harmonicas clasped around their necks. I struck up a conversation with a handsome, long-haired nineteen-year-old who was the local Casanova and fellow mutineer. Bill Miller was the guitar player of a resident band, the American Dream, and the entire lawless group lived in a six-story walk-up on Eighth Street.

I'd seen some funky places in my travels, but the East Village was a far cry from the sandy beaches and swaying palm trees in California. There was a bathtub in the kitchen that doubled as someone's bed, and a squalid communal toilet on the landing that didn't look too happy. Yikes, I'd never seen so many cockroaches!

Everyone was waiting for a guy they called the Chemist. He was bringing some crystal meth, whatever that was.

A shady-looking chap with a pocked complexion skulked in, shrouded in a dark overcoat, toting a black satchel. He poured a heap of sparkling white powder on the table, then scooped a bit into a crooked matchbook cover. He sprinkled the exotic dust into a glass of wine, and they passed the swill. Wanting to be cool, I couldn't very well say, "No thank you," so I swigged down the bitter brew with the rest of them, and literally couldn't shut my eyes for the next two days. On the second night I began to fret. I hadn't a clue what was in that glass. Would I ever be able to sleep again? My heart was thumping like a scared rabbit and my eyes looked like vapid dark moons. At dawn I dashed down the six flights to get a hot chocolate at Smiler's, the all-night deli, and was stopped in my tracks. There was a man lying as still as a rock on the grimy cold tiles. I thought, "Holy Jesus, a dead man!" I knelt down close to have a better look and almost fainted when he popped up like a jack-in-the-box. I rushed to the deli and bought him some hot coffee and a cherry Danish out of my bus money to help him recover from the blackout. I was worried about the old guy. When I told Bill about the man, he just laughed at my innocence about New York.

"He's a bum, they all sleep down there."

I had been in New York less then forty-eight hours and already had a rock-and-roll boyfriend, was high as the stars on speed, and was making friends with the neighborhood bums—not really what I had in mind.

While checking out my new neighborhood, I stumbled upon a wonderful little café on the corner of Bleecker and MacDougal. It was the Cafe Figaro, a raucous little hot spot with pretty street nymphs, brooding delinquent boys, and curious uptown slummers. At night there was wild dancing in the basement, and someone always seemed to have all the LSD we could swallow.

In that little Pandora's box I met some of my lifelong friends. There was fourteen-year-old Liz Argiss, whose mother worked for Revlon. Liz always had paper sacks full of surplus lipsticks and blush-on that she generously passed around so we could all look our prettiest. Then there was the beautiful little Patti D'Arbanville, with the blue eyes of an angel. At thirteen she already owned the hearts of all the boys, and she dreamed of becoming an actress. We were a fraternity of "little women" gone awry.

Liz wound up marrying rock guitarist Rick Derringer, and Patti still graces the silver screen.

I became fast friends with an uptown rich girl who rescued me from the ravages of Eighth Street and desolation row. Eileen Rubinstein was rail thin with perfect jet black, bobbed hair and a Picasso-looking angular face. She'd come dancing down at the Figaro, and always dressed to the nines. She had the latest in Betsey Johnson paraphernalia, and wore the most enviable, expensive shoes from Henri Bendel's. Eileen was seventeen, three years older than me. She lived with her divorced mother, whom she ran riot over, so there was no problem with me moving right in. She also had carte blanche with her dad's credit cards, and was happy to share the wealth. Miss Rubinstein introduced me to a whole new concept of what New York City had to offer.

Eileen taught me the art of applying false eyelashes and how to bind my blossoming boobs with Ace bandages so we could squeeze into form-fitting Mary Quant dresses. I was becoming glamorous. We'd go dancing till the wee hours at exclusive Arthur's or trendy Ondine, then on to a 5:00 A.M. breakfast at the Brasserie or the Click. I felt like a vampire seeing the sunrise. People were going to work as we hailed a cab in full glamour girl mod regalia, psychedelic satin skirts up to our teenage butts with vivid purple feather boas wafting in the early morning air. That was my new life: trendy discos and all-night dancing.

I was dancing the night away at Ondine when I met a beautiful boy with long blond curls and extraordinary style. He was dressed in the coolest striped-wool trousers, with an English schoolboy's jacket and a creamy cashmere scarf softly bundled around his neck.

Eric Emerson was a budding fashion designer and seemed a bit more sophisticated; he shined a little brighter than the other boys. He was a whimsical rogue with a seductive edge and a big capital T for trouble.

The Doors were onstage, and we danced like savages to Jim Morrison moaning, "Come on baby, light my fire." Later Eric asked if I wanted to go downtown to the Factory; Andy Warhol was having a bash. Before we caught a cab, Eric dashed to the men's room and returned.

"I just shot up some acid, you want to do some?"

Wow, shooting up LSD? I didn't even know you could do that! The last time a doctor had given me a shot I almost fainted, not to mention that injecting acid sounded insane.

"Can I just have a little from the bottle?"

I touched the tip of my tongue to the cap. By the time we got downtown, the cobblestone streets had turned into shimmmering rubies, sapphires, and deep green emeralds. I tried but couldn't extract a single stone.

The Factory was in an inconspicuous dingy warehouse on Forty-seventh Street, with a rickety service elevator and folding metal gates that opened directly onto the entire top floor, revealing a sea of dazzling, decadent revelers. It looked like a scene out of Fellini's *Juliet of the Spirits*. Sexy pretty boys who looked like girls danced with women resembling exotic birds. Even the not-so-pretty girls had a beauty and a grand style of their own. Andy's films were flickering on the walls, and I could hear the shattering drone of the Velvet Underground peaking in the distance. This was more than a mere party; it was an ongoing extraordinary lifestyle. I met *Cosmopolitan*'s cover photographer Francesco Scavullo, who said I should be a model and gave me his card. I danced with Nico, the seductive German singer in the Velvet Underground, and flirted with Lou Reed, the rake from the band. Most interesting of all, Andy himself asked if I'd like to come back. He wanted to take my picture.

So I returned to the Warhol kingdom. I hadn't noticed the night of the party, but in the daylight the Factory, in all its decadent glory, was entirely decked in silver, from floor to ceiling. Even the funky confined bathroom was papered in shiny aluminum foil and steeped in artful, pornographic graffiti.

Andy and his assistant, Paul Morrissey, were occupied releasing silver helium-filled pillows out of the bay windows into the city air. On the ratty sofa, the only existing piece of furniture in the studio, sat two beauties, the mysterious, blond Nico and the radiant actress Marisa Berenson. An artist, Ronnie Cutrone, was sloshing colors on a fresh canvas, and the painfully handsome playboy Baron François de Ménil was playing the Lovin' Spoonful's latest hit, "Do You Believe in Magic," over and over on a portable record player in the corner.

The afternoon was still young. Andy rigged a 16-millimeter camera a few feet from my face, then left me to wiggle and squirm in the close-up lens for what seemed like an hour. I think he later called these little films *Screen Tests*. As the day wore on the usual suspects straggled in, and the party started all over again.

The Factory was pretty wide open. There was no doorman or security. Basically, anyone was welcome, but if you didn't fit in, you quickly felt the chill.

Andy had an omnipotent presence, he was a sort of phantom, soft-spoken orchestrator who observed from a distance and always had a ready camera. In all the time I spent at the Factory I could never really tell what Andy looked like. He had created a character, an image that always looked curiously out of focus.

I spent most of the winter hanging out at the Factory and doing miscellaneous modeling assignments for the French magazine *Paris Match*. I'd been dying for the coveted, and regular, position as DJ at the infamous discotheque Ondine. The job paid fifty dollars a week, plus a gratis gourmet feast. When Billie, the regular disk spinner, took a leave, the job was mine.

Ondine was a completely different scene from Warhol's Factory; it was more rock-and-roll chic. The uptown disco was owned by fashion photographer Jerry Schatzberg, and was always abounding with leggy models, glamour girls, and handsome bad boys to match. Warren Beatty often held court with the ladies in the white leather booth next to the dance floor. You knew if the Stones or the Yardbirds were in town, they'd be at Ondine later in the night.

I ran into my friend Liz there, the little blond girl from the Village. She'd been hanging out with Denny Laine, the twenty-one-year-old singer from the Moody Blues, and she invited me to a little soiree for the band. Denny waltzed in late, clothed in an English-tailored black suit and Spanish-heeled Beatle boots. He looked like John Lennon with Paul McCartney's bedroom eyes. When he said, "Hello, love," in his soft English intonation, I was already envisioning us standing at the altar. This was the man who would change my life and give me my only son.

I went to every Moody Blues show and swooned when listening to Denny sing "Go Now" in his soulful timbre.

If sex was love, I'd fallen deep. I was still too inexperienced to gauge things like compatibility. All I knew about Denny was that he looked beautiful, sang in a rock band, and lived in England, and that there was a huge attraction. For a romance-minded teen, that was enough. In the beginning of our relationship I told Denny that I was almost eighteen, which was my usual stock answer. It was a far cry from a fifteen-year-old runaway delinquent from a pokey in California, not to mention the all points bulletin. When we were staying at his New York hotel I'd get up before dawn, lock myself in the bathroom, and reapply fresh, grown-up-looking makeup, with false eyelashes, sleek black eyeliner, and a touch of blush. Then I'd slip back to bed and pretend I had just woken up. He'd ask what I did so long in the bathroom. But he never questioned my age.

When the Moody Blues finished their New York engagement the band planned to take a holiday in Puerto Rico. Denny and I were in the throes of fresh young romance, and not yet ready to say good-bye. When I showed up on the Puerto Rican shoreline in a bathing suit the other members of the band went quiet. I may have fooled Denny, but in the bright sunlit beach I must have looked like underage veal. There was a Moody Blues meeting that night, something about me being a juvenile and Denny taking me out of the country. I was put on a plane the next day and sent back to New York City.

Denny said not to worry, I could come to England, but how was I going to get my fugitive hands on a legal passport? Denny went back and we kept the torch ablaze through wistful letters and expensive transatlantic phone calls. The week I turned sixteen I decided to chance my freedom and applied for a passport. All I needed was a letter of consent to travel alone, which I simply forged. I was on my way to England.

8

I could see Denny waiting just outside the glassed-in customs partition with an armful of flowers. Close to six months had passed, and he looked even more dazzling than I remembered. I felt a little woozy as the customs agent scrutinized my passport and counterfeit letter, then asked to see my return-trip ticket. What return ticket? I was staying forever. In a sternly British accent, he ordered, "Would you please step over to the side, Miss."

Oh, my God, I was going to be arrested, and there was no way out of it! Not only would I never see Denny again, but they were also going to call the authorities, locate my mother, and send me back to the tower. When the rest of the passengers filed through, Denny walked up. "What's the holdup, love?"

The officer cut in. "First off, she's underage, has no return ticket, and no verifiable residence. She can't be admitted into the country."

I was about to faint, when a magical thing happened: The customs agent recognized Denny. It turned out that he was a big fan of the

Moody Blues and had just seen him sing "Go Now" on *Top of the Pops*. Smiling, he gave me three months on my visa, and we were off.

We raced through the streets of London in Denny's little Mini Cooper, over the Putney Bridge to Carlisle Square.

London was a magical place. I loved the embellished architecture, gentle villages, and narrow cobblestone streets. The smells in the chemist's and small shops were comforting and familiar. I felt like I knew it here, like I'd come home after a long journey.

There was a stretch of King's Road in Chelsea that was like a wonderfully mysterious private club. It was the street where rock bands shopped, and prancing, long-legged models strutted in velvet miniskirts and colorful platform boots. There were outdoor cafés where all the boys resembled budding rock stars. My favorite place was the exclusive Chelsea Antique Market, which brimmed with lavish Victorian treasures. Upstairs a seductive Hungarian, Ulla, revamped faded silk gowns, fanciful French cravats, and embroidered piano shawls into whimsical, prismatic costumes. The top floor was a rooftop garden overlooking the King's Road, where you sipped tea and nibbled on sweet biscuits while watching the ongoing extravaganza. At the end of King's Road was a shop called Granny Takes a Trip. Its storefront was the back end of a car that looked like it had just crashed through the window. Granny's specialized in made-to-order velvet cowboy suits, handmade snakeskin boots, and skin-tight crushed-velvet trousers. Their calling card read, "Granny's makes clothes to wear before you make love." Talking 'bout my generation, this was a whole new era, and it was only the beginning.

Denny's flat was nothing as I'd imagined; it wasn't fancy or artsy, just a modern, ordinary apartment, comfortably cozy with a lovely green garden in the back.

The Beatles had just topped the charts with *Revolver* and we played "Here, There, and Everywhere" continually, like an anthem.

I had arrived at the height of the psychedelic, rock-and-roll revolution. It wasn't unusual to go to a party and see John Lennon or have a puff of pot with Paul McCartney. We went dancing with Ringo and Maureen, and spent a hallucinogenic night on acid with Brian Jones and his German girlfriend, Anita Pallenberg. I doted on Denny, cooking his dinner and pressing his trendy shirts. I thought we were happy, but it wasn't long before there was big trouble in paradise.

At sixteen I wasn't the best judge of emotions. I'd confused delirious teenage passion for everlasting love. As long as we were between the sheets, which was most of the time, we were snow-blind, but Denny was becoming increasingly moody (no pun intended), with a volatile, crazy jealousy. "But to love her is to need her everywhere" was more prophetic than I realized. It started off subtly, but I started to feel like a prisoner. I couldn't even go to the shops without him waiting at the door with jealous insinuations. He'd sometimes grapple me to the floor and trounce me to tears all because of his green-eyed imagination. Later on, he'd be repentant, and I so much wanted to believe him.

The elevated drama certainly kept the sex at a fevered pitch, but crazy drama was what I'd run away from in the first place. His jealousy was so out of control, he once chased a passing bus halfway down the block when a guy whistled at me from the platform. I began walking with my head down just to keep the peace. To make matters worse, Denny decided it was a good time to quit the Moody Blues. With no work and too much time for nothing, he fell into a dark depression that I couldn't penetrate.

Living with him became like trying to avoid an approaching wreck. It seemed no matter what I did or said, I couldn't make Denny believe I loved him. I was in a tangle of mixed-up feelings; was love supposed to hurt? Denny was my first real home, and the only security I'd ever known. I didn't want to leave, but I knew I couldn't stay. I tearfully abandoned my raging bull and headed back to New York City.

I moved back in with my friend Eileen Rubinstein, and we picked up right where we left off, haunting the discos and dancing till dawn. I still missed Denny, and had mixed feelings about leaving him. I think it was more the dreamy idea of being in love, or the fact that somebody loved me. I was still only sixteen, parading as a grownup, trying to survive. I had my hard-fought freedom, but I was pretty much alone in the world.

In the meantime the infamous DJ Murray the K was promoting a ten-day rock show at the Academy of Music on 58th Street. The headliners were Mitch Ryder & the Detroit Wheels, Smokey Robinson & the Miracles, Wilson Pickett, and the Blues Project. Smokey begged out at the last minute, but the big hoopla was about two new debuting bands from England, the Who and Cream. My pretty black girlfriend Emeretta, who could charm her way into Fort Knox, suggested we go check it out. Maybe we could see some of the acts. We slipped in the backstage door just in time to see the first rehearsal. It was the gorgeous, blond Roger Daltrey singing the incendiary "My Generation." We lucked out; there wasn't a sign of security, and besides the bands, there was not a soul in the auditorium. We made a dash for the back-row seats and watched history explode.

As Pete Townshend wielded his guitar, shattering it against a wall of speakers, Eric Clapton came in and took the seat right next to me. Keith Moon was smashing his drums all over the stage like a bar brawl, then lit the whole lot on fire—and this was just the rehearsal. It was the Who's and Cream's inaugural appearance, and Emeretta and I were their first and only audience.

Eric Clapton was beyond cool in his British, purple-velvet trousers and snakeskin boots; you couldn't get that kind of finery in America, which made him seem all the more mysterious. Eric asked if I was going to stay to see his band, and invited Emeretta and me backstage after the rehearsal. We became fast friends with the English invaders, and attended every performance. There were five separate shows a day, starting at an unbelievable 10:30 A.M. Cream only had enough time to do "I Feel Free" and "I'm So Glad," and the Who ended the show with "My Generation." I was having great fun hanging with the British rockers. Little did I know that in the not so distant future I'd be moving in with Eric Clapton, singing onstage with Ginger Baker, and that Roger Daltrey would become one of my dearest, lifelong friends.

Since I'd returned from England, something didn't feel right. I felt dizzy and listless, and the slightest scent of perfume made me feel oddly nauseated. As the weeks went by the smell of food, or even the sound of someone's breath, sent me retching to the toilet. I thought it was just a stubborn strain of Asian flu, and vomited ten pounds off before consulting with a doctor. It hadn't even occurred to me that I might be pregnant, but the doctor surprised me with the stunning confirmation. I was going to have a baby. I'd been wanting a child of my own since I was old enough to remember, but my current circumstances didn't feel like the best situation to bring a new soul into the world. When I called Denny he couldn't have been happier. He said to come back, that things would be better now.

I felt as if I'd been scooped up by a cresting wave that I had to ride out, but the truth was that I loved Denny when he was rational. Perhaps a baby would make things better.

Denny had formed the Electric String Band, a classical-meets-rock outfit, with a string quartet from the London Royal Academy. His new band was gaining notoriety with the critics, and we were getting on so well that we decided to tie the knot. We dressed up in our finest clothes, Denny in his svelte tailored suit and psychedelic shimmer shirt, and I, seven months pregnant, in a satin pale pink minidress and silver knee-high platform boots. We strolled hand in hand down King's Road to the registrar's office, but it had closed early that day.

After another show of rage, Denny wrote me a love song called "Say You Don't Mind." I think it was his way of saying he was sorry. The sad little ditty, "I've been doing some growing, now I'm scared that you're going," captured my mixed-up teenage heart again—and also made it to the English Hit Parade. Next came "Catherine's Wheel." Did all best love songs come from real-life anguish?

I was distraught and now too pregnant to go anywhere; my baby would soon be born in Kensington at Saint Mary Abbot's hospital.

My young friend Heather Taylor, a red-haired model who I used to go dancing with at Ondine in New York, had come to London to rendezvous with the guitar virtuoso from the Yardbirds, Jimmy Page. Heather was a statuesque six-foot beauty with exquisite style and a healthy appreciation for bad boys. Jimmy, with his ethereal, almost frail manner and soft black ringlets falling around his pale skin, was the ultimate in heartache.

Sadly, after just three dreamy dates with her he expressed, in his sweetest tone, that perhaps they were seeing too much of each other. Besides being devastated, Heather was stuck miles away from London, living with her gran in the English countryside. I still had Roger Daltrey's London phone number from New York, and knowing his kind heart and adoration of beautiful women I had an idea.

"Why don't you call Roger. I'll bet you could stay with him."

Heather took my advice, and five years later they were married.

My relationship with Denny was disintegrating quickly. We were getting along like a pair of Japanese fighting fish. In my last month of pregnancy, he'd often smoke hash into oblivion, then sleep it off on the sofa. One frosty November morning, as I was getting ready for my prenatal appointment at Saint Mary's, I stood a little too close to the fireplace. With a frightening swoosh, my flowing Victorian nightgown burst into blazes. I could hear my long locks sizzling up my back as I tried to get the fragile, flaming gown off over my head.

Denny was out cold on the sofa while I ran around in circles like a lit torch, trying to pat out the flames. I finally screamed, "Denny, help, I'm on fire!"

He was up like a shot, wrapping me in his blanket, patting me down, and professing his love for me. As soon as the flames were snuffed, he reproached me for his blistered hands and went back to his sleep. I felt the baby kicking around in my belly and questioned myself. "What was I thinking when I made the decision to have a child with this man?"

I'd read every book I could find on childbirth, and knitted, crocheted, and embroidered enough booties and bonnets to outfit an entire maternity ward. When the labor pains began at 7:00 A.M., I must have read the childbirth chapter twenty times over. I called the hospital, but they said it wasn't time yet. How would I know when it's time? By midnight I was restless, and the pains were hard to ignore. Oddly, Denny seemed oblivious to what was about to happen.

I called Heather and Roger for some words of comfort, but there was no answer, so I dialed an ambulance to take me to Saint Mary's. By now the labor pains were so intense I was in a state of delirium. Denny followed the ambulance to the hospital, but a nun told him it would be awhile, that he should go home and get some sleep. Saint Mary Abbots was an old Victorian hospital, almost Dickensian. In some of the corridors original gaslight fixtures still hung from the walls. The nurses were nuns and dressed in traditional long black habits. Some wore wide, crisp white wimples that tipped up on the sides. Two sisters wheeled me on a gurney into a small, dimly lit room, then disappeared for what felt like eternity. I could hear the other expectant mothers laboring in the ward. Their woeful, resonant howls echoed throughout the early morning halls. That wasn't going to be me. I would be brave.

I remember calmly calling out in vain, "Hello, Doctor? Sister? Can anyone hear me? I think the baby's coming."

I hadn't a clue where I was or if anyone was even out there. Every few hours a hasty nun would enter my room and briskly force my legs apart. She'd prod around my insides, tell me I wasn't ready yet, and then disappear back into the shadows. Later I was startled by a close, plaintive scream, then recognized that it was coming from me. I'd finally succumbed. It felt as if hungry beasts were feasting on my insides, ripping and gnawing deep down, from the inside out. The shattering torture went on well into the late morning. I don't know if painkillers were even an option, but no one was offering.

I don't recall being wheeled to the operating room, but in my hazy, half-crazed state I heard a male voice telling me to "push." With his shoulder-length blond hair he looked way too young to be the physician. He sat perched between my legs, shouting, "Push, push harder," as an unfamiliar midwife held on to my teenage hand. After thirty sleepless, nonstop hours of writhing agony, on November 27, 1967, the mystery doctor held my baby high, and exclaimed, "You have a son." That was just what I wanted. He rested the baby in my arms, and I wept with joyous bliss. Denny arrived on the dot of visiting hours, bearing a bouquet of fresh-cut pink roses, and for that moment life appeared to be perfect.

Heather was my second visitor, and she made a splash in the drab, prewar maternity ward, gliding in wearing full Edwardian regalia. Her floor-length orange velvet cloak shimmered and billowed along with her elegant gait. She wore an antique jeweled band around her sumptuous flowing red hair. Victorian lace and tiny embroidered red roses peeked up through the rouched collar of her cape. Heather always looked like a John Waterhouse pre-Raphaelite princess. She said she was off to a party, but she always dressed that way. In honor of the new little life, she brought me a delicate, amethyst necklace from the Chelsea Antique Market, then she was off to the ball.

At this time in England it was required for a new mother to remain in the hospital for a full ten days after giving birth. Denny never missed a visiting day, but two days before I was released, the Electric String Band were scheduled to play a show in Scotland. Denny wouldn't be back till the next night, so I had to take a taxi with my new baby back to our flat. It felt surreal walking out of the hospital with this tiny infant all on my own. I was just seventeen, and now someone's mother. I managed to make it back to Chelsea safely and set the baby in his waiting cot. When he began to fuss I thought he must be hungry so I put him to my breast like the sister had showed me at Saint Mary's, and it worked like a charm. I gave him a warm bath, brushed the feathery wisps on his delicate head, then swaddled him in the pale blue angora blanket I'd crocheted for him. I spent the rest of the night staring in wonderment at this fragile new life. What an adventure we would have.

As unique and original as the Electric String Band's music was, they never really took off. Denny was still struggling, and we were poor as church mice. We were getting along somewhat better, but his dark, dismal moods still lurked and loomed. He often sat silently in despair with his head in his hands for hours. When Heather, my sole friend, would come for a visit, he'd go in the bedroom and fling the door shut behind him. I was a happy-natured girl with an angelic new baby. I loved Denny and I knew he loved me, but his depression was bewildering. It was like living in a dense fog that smothered any sense of joy. It wasn't a flip or easy decision, but I didn't see any happiness in our future. I decided to pack up baby Damian and went to stay with Roger and Heather at Saint John's Wood. Roger gave us the top floor in his homey brownstone, and fashioned a cozy bed for baby Damian out of an antique dresser drawer. The four of us were a happy house, but I knew I couldn't stay on with them forever. It was time to make a life myself. Denny sent me letters and called, appealing for me to come home. He wanted to get married, for real this time, and make it legitimate. Whenever I'd try to leave, Denny had a way of turning back into the man I had fallen in love with. Seeing him sweet and vulnerable had always made me forget, but not this time. I was taking my six-month-old Damian Christian and going home, back to California.

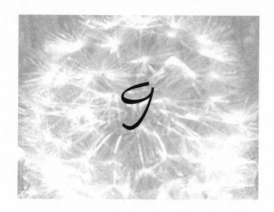

I had written to my grandmother but hadn't seen Mimi since I was fourteen, the night I'd kissed her sweet cheek good-bye at the institution. What an adventure I'd had since then! It was already 1967. In three short years, I'd lived in San Francisco, Boston, New York, and London. I'd even been to Puerto Rico with Denny! I'd hung out with Andy Warhol, and now had a child of my own. I could see that coming home with a baby was somewhat bittersweet. Actually, I think she was mortified. I knew she'd wanted more for me, like a proper education or at least an adoring husband, but in grand Mimi style she only scolded: "I was worried, love; I missed you."

It didn't take long for her to fall in love with her new great-grandson, and as always she was there like an angel to simplify and bolster my seemingly impractical lifestyle.

With Mimi's help I rented the bottom half of a Craftsman house on Bronson Avenue by the Hollywood sign. We combed the thrift shops for mismatched furniture and bits of curtain lace. For the first time I held a key to my very own place.

The woman upstairs had lived there since the house was built, and for five dollars a night she became my trusted babysitter. I got a job selling tickets in the admittance booth at a riotous little nightclub called the Experience on the Sunset Strip. I'd hitchhike five miles to work, then get a late-night ride home from Marshall Brevets, the frenzied owner of the club.

The Experience was the perfect name for this little beehive of incredible music. For two dollars you could see anyone from Chuck Berry to Jimi Hendrix. There was B. B. King, T.Rex, and even a young Alice Cooper gracing the stage. One summer night Bo Diddley walked his whole band off the set and finished his show on the sidewalk on Sunset Boulevard. A bearded and bloated Jim Morrison often stumbled onto the intimate stage and harassed other bands. In his drunkenness he'd take over the microphone, wailing obscenities till he was gently removed from the premises. The local bands reigned supreme, and wreaked wild havoc with loose young women in the shadows. It was so dark in there, you never knew what was going on.

When I was a child, my grandfather had teased me, "When you grow up, the boys are going to be lining up at your door with mattresses on their backs."

I had envisioned a queue of men lugging cumbersome beds to my front door, but I didn't get the joke. As it turned out, he was right. I certainly had my share of admirers. Love notes sailed though my windows in the form of paper airplanes, and I received so many bouquets and baskets of flowers my house looked like I was hosting a wake. With all my young suitors, there was only one who just about charmed the panties off me. I met Roman Polanski at a dinner party in Malibu, and there was instant attraction. At the end of the evening he asked for my phone number, and called the next afternoon. Roman didn't actually call himself; he summoned his secretary to ask if I was free to have dinner. I thought it odd that he'd have his secretary telephone.

"Why doesn't he call for himself?"

Five minutes later the phone rang again, and I made plans to dine with the engaging Mr. Polanski. He swooped me up in a black Rolls-Royce, and we went to a cozy little bistro, the Black Rabbit on Robertson. Although Roman was twice my age, he didn't look much older than the other boys I dated. He was elegant, cultivated, and comfortable to be with. Over a softly lit dinner, I spoke a little of my young life, and then Roman went on to tell me how he had survived growing up in Poland during the war, and how his mother died in a concentration camp. My eyes started to well with tears; he was the real deal. My tales of woe were trivial in comparison. On our next date he took me to Malibu, where he was staying. We had an early dinner, then went to the movies to see Arlo Guthrie in *Alice's Restaurant*. It was late when the film let out.

"Why don't you just spend the night," he suggested.

He said he had to be at Paramount in the morning, so it would be easier to drop me off then. Nope, I insisted, I had to get home and pick up my baby son.

"Well, then," he said, "if you don't want to stay over, why don't you take my car back to town; I can pick it up tomorrow."

Little did Mr. Polanski know, I hadn't a clue how to drive a car. The only thing I'd ever driven were the kiddie cars in the safe confines of the Autopia ride at Disneyland. Still, I took him up on his brave offer.

"Let's take a little drive around the parking lot, see how you go." Right away, my inexperience was apparent.

"That's unusual, you use separate feet for the gas and brakes?"

"Oh, yeah, I always do," I giggled.

Fortunately the car was an automatic, and I managed to lunge and lurch myself all the way back to Hollywood.

My little house on Bronson was becoming quite the rock-and-roll hangout, and it rang with unique music well into the Hollywood nights. Eric Clapton gave me a Guild guitar for my eighteenth birthday and taught me the chords to "Badge." Jimi Hendrix would call asking, in his reticent manner, "This is Jimi . . . would you mind . . . would it be okay if I stopped by for a while?"

I think he needed some solitude, a place to hide from the women who brazenly hunted him. He always had a guitar in hand, and I'd ask, "Would you play 'Little Wing,' and show me the chords?"

I had plenty of handsome suitors, but no one really had my heart until I encountered the ethereal Jimmy Page. Heather had given me a pretty accurate description, but there were no real words to describe his seductive allure and painful charm. It wasn't just his lithe, elegant, rock-and-roll mien, or his pre-Raphaelite angelic face and soft long curls. He had an indescribable smoldering look in his eyes, like he had a secret he might share with you one day. When we kissed he inhaled my breath like he was savoring my soul. I'd never felt anything quite as dark or sensuous as James Patrick Page. He captivated me with stories of the English countryside and his lone manor in Pangbourne surrounded by a majestic moat. He always made me feel like we were somewhere off in the mists of Avalon.

Although he hadn't exactly spoken the words, he did some heavy alluding. I had illusive visions of being the blithe young maiden of the manor; we'd give life to a band of seraphim and be eternally happy. Little did I know several other girls were under the same identical spell.

Jimmy was still playing guitar with the Yardbirds, but he was also working on putting his own group together in England. He said he was hoping to come back to California soon. If the band did well, then they'd do a West Coast tour. Obviously it went quite well, because Led Zeppelin hit Los Angeles like napalm. After their dazzling debut at the Whisky A-Go-Go, Led Zeppelin became the new rock-and-roll gods. Jimmy stayed at my house for the first two luminous nights, then the band went up to San Francisco for more accolades at the Fillmore.

The next thing I knew Jimmy had disappeared. I heard he was holed up at the Hyatt House on Sunset with one of Frank Zappa's infamous G.T.O.'s (Girls Together Outrageously) and Hollywood's chief groupie, Miss Pamela. My romantic teenage heart was shattered. I agonized, longed, and generally stirred myself into a state.

In the midst of my misery, while still working at the Experience, a most beautiful boy came in wanting to buy a ticket for B.B. King. Because the show was almost over I told him he could go in for free, but he didn't budge. He just stood there, staring with the sweetest smile and most soulful brown eyes. I felt an electric jolt in my heart and could almost see the fairy dust falling around me.

"What time do you get off?"

I still had half an hour to go but replied, "Right now."

I was wearing a white summer minidress and my sexy new platform slides. When I came around the corner, he looked at my long legs and breathed an audible sigh. As we walked to a café down the boulevard I could feel the sweet thunder shimmer between us.

Jackson Browne was a yet unrecognized songwriter who lived in the hills of Echo Park. "Would you like to come over and hear some of my songs?"

It didn't take much persuasion, and we were off in his faded-blue Volkswagen.

His apartment was part of an old house nestled in the hills of Echo Park overlooking the Lake. It was sparsely furnished, just a simple bed, dresser, a few tables, and an old upright piano in the living room. Jackson's house had the feeling of a monk's quarters, clean and calm, with smooth hardwood floors. The only decorative touches were a lovely old silk embroidered crazy quilt his grandmother had stitched, a holy crucifix on the wall, and a vase of fading wildflowers on the windowsill.

Jackson sat down at the piano and played a slow-moving version of "Doctor My Eyes." The rendering was so beautiful it gave me a chill. By the last longing note of "Jamaica Say You Will" I was full of desire. I wanted to be Jamaica and make love in the shadow of the tall green grass. We didn't even kiss that night, but the anticipation was heavenly. The night was sweeter than a kiss. I could have stayed all night and just gazed into his deep brown eyes till the dawn, but I had to get home to collect my boy from the babysitter.

After meeting Jackson it didn't take long to forget about Jimmy's swift departure. I was quickly under the spell of Jackson's gentle heart. He was tender with baby Damian, and took us out on lovely little outings. We'd go boating on the lake by his house and take long walks up to the stream at Bronson Park. One of my favorite places was the historical abbey. It was in Highland Park, and his grandfather had built it in 1925. It was the place where Jackson had lived as a boy, and looked like a magical small-scale Gothic castle. Then there was his impassioned music that captivated me.

Jackson wrote me a song called "Under the Falling Sky." One of the verses was, "Abandon your sad history and meet me in the fire."

Into the fire we went. The chemistry between Jackson and me was like a magnet to metal. We could barely look at each other without falling into bed. We christened every room in the house, the Volkswagen, and even a public dressing room when we were out shopping. We could never get close enough. The soft smell of his freshly washed damp hair, his taste, and his breathtaking long hands, the sharp line of his jaw, his voice, and his music, it all sent me.

Jackson was hired to sing at a folk club just outside San Francisco, and we decided to make a little holiday of it. Mimi agreed to look after Damian, and we tooled our way up north in his VW bug. One of his friends had offered to let us stay at a lovely farmhouse in the country. We took the cozy room on the top floor, and we spent the weekend lost in young abandoned passion. It felt like we were worldly old souls, but I was barely nineteen and he was only twenty-one years old.

Jackson was still relatively unknown, but when we arrived at the coffeehouse the small venue had standing room only. It was packed full with adoring followers. As he sang "A Song for Adam" he was aglow in amber stage light, and you could just about hear a feather fall. At that moment I thought we would be together forever.

I became completely wrapped up in the warm romance of Jackson Browne. My son had just learned to walk and I had my own place and interesting employment. My life seemed to be taking a gentle form, until I received an ill-fated call. My girlfriend Lorraine, who was married to Traffic's Dave Mason, had just returned from England. She said she'd spent some time with Denny Laine, and had given him my address and telephone number. I hadn't seen Denny for more than a year, nor had I really thought of him. At first I ignored his letter, but then hearing his soft English voice over the long-distance wire was hard to dismiss. He said he missed our son and how he'd had time to think and change his reckless ways. He'd even started his own publishing company and called it Naimad, which is Damian spelled backward. He'd also joined a new band with Ginger Baker called Air Force, and had plenty of money to take care of us now. He wanted another chance. I'd been with Jackson for almost a whole dreamy year. How quickly I forgot my prior despair. After a few months of cloak-and-dagger sweet talk and hopeful promises, I found myself thinking, "Maybe he really did change." He was the father of my son. But how was I going to tell Jackson I was moving back to England?

I waited till the last possible moment to mention it, but even then I had a grim feeling in my soul. Why was I doing this? Jackson, always the gentleman, saw Damian and me off at the British Airways terminal. At the gate he handed me an antique velvet doll's slipper stuffed with a delicate quail egg, which I still possess. I knew I was about to board an enormous mistake. I wanted to turn back and go home, but it was too late. I'd let go of my house, our bags were packed, and the jumbo jet plane was ready for take-off.

For the first few months it seemed my hasty choice had actually been the right decision. The three of us, a family, were living together in a rambling two-story Tudor in the sleepy village of Cholesbury. Denny doted on Damian, and even bought me a vintage Jaguar XK 150 convertible to motor around the village in. It was like we'd fallen in love all over again. Everything was perfect, except for one little catch. The lovely old house in all its country splendor was a prewar Tudor, built well before the days of central heating. There were five bedrooms, a formal dinning room, and a grand-sized living room with a hearthstone so wide you could actually sit in it. Granted, there was a fireplace in each room, but unless you stood close to the flame, the rooms were so chilly, it felt like it might snow in the house. I spent most of my days lugging cumbersome buckets of heavy coal, logs, and kindling up two flights of stairs. I stoked waning embers with antique bellows, and boiled huge pots of water on the wood-burning auger just to have a lukewarm bath. We were freezing our butts off. I begged Denny, "Could we please get a smaller place with some heat?"

We ended up keeping the house in the country, but also rented a toasty furnished flat in London. It was the ground floor of a brownstone in the ritzy area of Kensington. The flat had a charming English garden, and was within walking distance to the famous Harrod's, my favorite department store.

Ginger Baker was looking for another backup singer for his band Air Force, and I asked if I might try out for the job. I'd always dreamed of singing. I loved the blues and Irish lilts, but rock and roll would do.

I auditioned for Ginger with an a cappella version of Billie Holiday's "My Man." And just like that I was signed up with the band. Soon after my audition, Air Force began a one-month tour of England. The whole band traveled the countryside in a magical mystery tour bus.

What an amazing life I seemed to be living. At twenty I was in a rock and roll band, singing at all the music festivals along with Jimi Hendrix, Eric Clapton, Richie Havens, Donovan, and all the other peerless bands of the sixties, plus getting paid as well. I had a proper English nanny for Damian, and a house in the country and one in London. I'd signed with a label—the Robert Stigwood organization—and we were recording an album. I had more cash than I could spend. I had become one of the mysterious girls on the King's Road, prancing in my silver platform boots, sheer chiffon minidresses, and feathers trailing in the English breeze.

Despite living in the rock-and-roll hurricane, I was miserable. Since we'd moved to London, Denny was slowly slipping back into his suspicious, morose mode. We were back to square one; the only difference was that we had money to burn. I missed California, my little house, Mimi, and Jackson's gentle way with me. I realized I'd made a huge mistake. If only I could click my heels and be back in my own little bed in Hollywood. I began to realize Denny's spontaneous rage wasn't going to magically disappear, nor did it have anything to do with me. It was simply his stormy nature, and it seemed he was never going to change. The teenage sexual obsession that had kept us together was all but gone. There was nothing sexy or attractive about being accused and threatened, nor did I want my innocent child to witness that sort of behavior.

Air Force was about to embark on an American tour. As everyone in the band had a fear of flying, the whole group was booked for passage on the QE2. We were packed and ready to sail, but the night before departure, the tour was canceled. Ginger decided he would prefer to go to Africa and play drums with the Nigerians. It seemed the band was finished. To tell you the truth, it was actually a relief; Denny and I had been booked in the same berth on the ship, and more than likely would have killed each other.

My friend Ned Doheny had just arrived in England from California and graciously called to say an innocent hello. Denny never liked it when I chatted on the phone, but this time he got so enraged that he cuffed me. The sheer impact sent me flying across the living room, delivering me to the corner in a dazed heap. I was so stunned I actually saw perfect five-point stars circling above my head, just like in the cartoons.

When I came to I saw a reflection of myself in the mirror. My entire face was covered in sticky crimson blood. I flew to the bathroom and locked the door. Denny stood outside apologizing and pleading for me to let him in. I found a deep gash just above my eye. Inspecting it closer in the mirror, I could see the skin was broken in a V shape with a jagged edge. I wasn't sure if it was Denny's silver ring or if I'd hit my head on the corner of the counter. I couldn't stop the bleeding, so I grabbed a towel and pressed it hard to my eye.

I needed to get to a hospital fast, and I didn't want that crazy man anywhere near me. I escaped out the bathroom window and scaled a steep wall along the side of our flat just to get to the street. A passing taxi saw my bloody plight and sped me to the hospital at no charge. When I got to St. George's, it took six unsightly black stitches to close the gaping wound. The initial adrenaline was beginning to wear off, and I was sniffling back my tears. I could hear the eerie sound of the sewing thread tensing through the skin above my eyelid, and thanked God I wasn't accidentally blinded. When the doctor was finished he handed me a mirror to have a look at his needle work. The crisscross sutures made me look like a sword-wielding pirate, but the worst was over. I was still recovering on the gurney when a nurse came in and told me my husband and son were in the waiting room. She said that if I didn't want to see them I could take the side passage out, and I took her advice.

For my final hurrah and last night in England, I met with some friends down at the "Speak." The Speakeasy was the definitive in-crowd rock-and-roll oasis. You walked down a flight of red-carpeted stairs and through a hallway that opened into a big comfy room with elevated levels and cloistered private booths. There was a stage where on any given night you could see Jimi Hendrix, Eric Clapton, the Small Faces, or Johnny and Edgar Winter performing beyond the dance floor. To the right was a raised-glassed partitioned restaurant where they served the best creamed petit pois and filet mignon sandwiches on the planet. You might find Rod Stewart or David Gilmour from Pink Floyd having a late-night meal, or catch a yet unknown David Bowie prancing on the crowded dance floor. Luigi, the tuxed Italian maître d', serendipitously sat me directly across from Eric Clapton, who was bemused by the sight of my freshly sewn sutures.

"What happened to you?" he asked.

I told him the whole grisly story, and that I was taking a flight home to California the following morning.

"Don't go back," he said. "Why don't you and Damian come and stay at Hertwood Edge for the summer?"

Eric had my trunks picked up from Kensington, and my son and I were off on our way to Surrey.

Hertwood Edge was Eric's country estate. His two-story manor had marble floors, wainscoted walls, and a dining room with French doors that looked out onto the lush English countryside. It was a formal Moorish manor, but not ritzy or bedecked, just comfortable and relaxed, with a pair of frisky dogs that had the run of the house. The grounds were beautiful, partly manicured but mostly wild, and they went on as far as you could see. Damian was happy there as well. He had free run of the house, but mostly enjoyed riding his tricycle up and down the wide halls.

Eric had just formed Derek and the Dominos, and for that summer the entire band hung out and did nothing but create heavenly music at all hours of the day and night. It was the onset of the *Layla* album, and you could feel the anguish in the air. Eric was despondently in love with Patti Boyd, but also close with Patti's husband, George Harrison. There was a feel of Shakespearean tragedy brewing in the manor. Eric was already a bit of a brooding wraith, but now painfully obsessed with winning Patti's hand. It seemed Patti could never find the right moment to break the news of their secret affair to George, which kept Eric in tormented uncertainty. Out of all the grief came the radiant song "Layla."

It was amazing to listen as Eric worked on pieces of music for the album, and going to the recording sessions that went on till dawn. I remember driving back to Eric's from a "Layla" recording session in London. I was with Bobby Whitlock, a member of Eric's band, and he was breaking in his brand-new Ferrari. The sun was just rising and

Bobby was doing an easy 130 miles an hour on the forest-lined motorway. There was a light mist in the air, and as we came over a small crest the Ferrari spun out of control. It spun five times across the road in eerie slow motion, then deposited us in a soft grassy patch in the woods. That was about as close to curtains as I'd ever come. Neither of us said a word. Bobby just started the Ferrari back up and we took off like bats out of hell. That's how it was back then—we all thought we were invincible.

I never missed a rehearsal, which could be heard the next village over. At the time it didn't really occur to me how special it was living at Eric's house, being a part of that extraordinary musical history. I was happy just being there.

As the only girl in residence, I became the household cook, and always had something tasty simmering on the stove. I got my secret recipes from Alice's Restaurant's cookbook, which had the yummiest hot chili to date. There was always plenty of hash to smoke, and the occasional Mandrax. "Mandies" were a dreamier, British version of quaaludes, like a quaalude lite. One night the dealer who usually brought hash and the Mandies arrived with something special. He called it "China white." I don't think any of us had ever tried heroin before. It was "Ooh, heroin, definitely taboo." We didn't even know how much to take.

After I'd moved in with Eric the impassioned drama between Denny and me had cooled. I wasn't going back, but Denny still wanted to stay close with our son. We agreed that Denny would have Damian on the weekends, and during the week he'd be with me at Hurtwood Edge. It was a Friday night; Damian was in London with Denny, so I was free to indulge. Eric and some of the other people in the house, including myself, all took the plunge and sniffed the white dust up our noses through a rolled-up ten-pound note. The four of us sat on the sofa in front of the fireplace in an utter, comatose silence, like we were asleep, but not quite. I remember trying to imagine the worst possible scenario. I thought about losing my child, my life, overdosing, but nothing seemed to faze me. Not even engulfing flames could get me to stir from the enveloping comfort of that couch. I was in essence dead with vital signs. I wouldn't be doing that again.

There was a party at Eric's house on July 14. It was a birthday bash for Jim Gordon, the drummer of the Dominos. George and Patti Harrison arrived together, and Mick Jagger showed up in his glistening white Bentley convertible. Mick had visited once before. I remember being engrossed in a book in the study when he peeked in and said, "You're pretty." With a blush, all I could think to say was a faint "thank you," and went back to reading my book.

George had just written "My Sweet Lord" and wanted to play it for Eric. As he played, the whole band joined in, and it sounded like music from the heavens. Someone had spiked the punch with mescaline, which made it sound all the more glorious. I was starting to feel pretty psychedelic, and thought I'd better call Denny and say good night to my son while I could still dial the phone. I went into the study next to the living room, and the walls were vibrating with the electric resonance of "My Sweet Lord" echoing throughout the house. As I was speaking with Denny, Mick came into the room and closed the door behind him. I was seated at the desk in a regal, antique high-back chair with ornate carved arms. Mick walked up next to me and just stood there. He was wearing these delicious black-and-white checkered houndstooth wool trousers with a soft cotton white shirt. When I looked over, all I could see was the undulating moving pattern of the houndstooth. Mick didn't say a word, but I felt the intensity. He was clearly waiting for me to get off the phone.

Abruptly, I said to Denny, "Okay, I have to go now, 'bye."

It was just a few months after Mick's starring role in Donald Cammell's film *Performance*. He was just twenty-six years old and at the height of his unbelievable stunningness.

By now we were both pretty high from the mescaline, and the anticipation of the kiss was almost unbearable. Mick eased me back against the wall, kissing me with a kind of abandon girls only dream about. Just like in a steamy romance novel, we slid down the wall in slow motion, lost in dreamy liquid kisses. By the time we reached the floor "My Sweet Lord" sounded like it was coming through the wall. I was definitely having a *stunning moment.*

When the music started to wane Mick and I composed ourselves, and slipped out to explore Eric's extensive garden grounds. We passed his guitar-shaped swimming pool, and farther down the path we found a lovely little spot with an old vine-covered trellis, and a bench just wide enough for two. It was a warm moonlit summer night, and like a couple of teenagers we kissed till the shape was worn from my lips. By the time we got back to the house it was past four in the morning, and everyone was off on their own trip or had gone back to London.

Watching Mick pull out of the driveway looking like some kind of dreamy god, I thought, "Is this really happening?" Yes, it was. Mick called the next day and invited Eric and me to see Stevie Wonder perform in London over the weekend.

For the event I wore my long, whimsical, gypsy dress from the posh Ozzie Clark's boutique. The velvet bodice was formfitting, buttoning down to a billowing skirt of colored silk layers. My pale pink platform boots with appliquéd silver crescent moons and stars from Granny Takes a Trip went perfectly with my outfit. Stevie Wonder was the hottest ticket in town, and I felt like a female divinity sitting between Mick and Eric, taking in Mr. Wonder's stellar performance.

On Mick's twenty-seventh birthday Patti Boyd came up to Eric's estate, and the two of us spent the afternoon scouting the countryside

in her red Mercedes convertible. We were checking out antique shops
in search of the perfect gift for Mick. We settled on a floral Victorian
animatronic bird sanctuary. It was enclosed in a large oval glass
bubble, and when you wound it up, tiny finches sang and fluttered
their feathered wings.

Mick's birthday party was at his four-story brownstone on Cheyne
Walk in Chelsea. I rode in from the country with Eric and Bobby
Whitlock. Patti Harrison had already arrived and was holding court in
the first-floor parlor. All the boys were drooling, with lust in their eyes.
With barely a hint of makeup and her blond locks casually pinned up,
Patti looked like a goddess. Mick, in all his splendidness, was upstairs
in the main parlor along with Keith Richards, Charlie Watts, and the
new Stone, Mick Taylor. The esoteric film director Kenneth Anger
and his demonic lot were lying back on some Indian cushions, smoking
spliffs of hash in the corner of the room. Mick came over with his boyish smile, as if he'd been waiting for me, and sweetly held my hand. He
introduced me to Donald Cammell and his sexy French girlfriend,
Myrium. Then he took me on a tour of his Chelsea brownstone.

On the third floor was the master bedroom, all candlelit and decked
in lavish antique Moroccan, complete with pillows, tassels, mirrors,
and an ornately carved four-poster bed. You could draw the weighty
velvet drapes completely around the bed and be cloaked in darkness.
Janice, his spirited young cook, had bought him silver satin sheets for
his birthday, and the bed was invitingly turned down. Mick brought
out a box that he'd brought from Morocco. The box contained three
rings, and he asked me to choose one. I picked the one that had a crescent moon and stars etched in amber, and he slid it on my middle finger. Ah, I thought, perhaps I would sleep in his lord's chamber tonight.

I did sleep in Mick's bed that night. The feelings and passion were
as dreamy as any romantic-minded girl might imagine. I remember his

kiss. It was like tasting something I couldn't get enough of, like the steamiest liquid kisses you ever saw on the silver screen.

After that night I pretty much moved right in. Master Damian had his own little nursery on the top floor, which had formerly accommodated Marianne Faithfull's son, Nicholas. Mick liked having a child in the house, and because of Damian's cherubic face and golden ringlets, he would sweetly comment, "Your son looks like you found him under a mulberry bush."

In the evenings after a romantic dinner at the fancy Mr. Chow's, or at some unknown hideaway, we'd go for long walks through the provinces of Chelsea. Mick was passionate about architecture and would tell tales, historic accounts of the aged dwellings and quaint carriage houses. He knew all the history, when the homes were built and what famous person or artists had lived in them. My favorite was the pre-Raphaelite artist Dante Gabriel Rossetti, who kept goats and other beasts in his abode.

Back at home we'd sip champagne and listen to obscure recordings. Mick loved Gram Parsons and Stephen Stills, and turned me on to blues accordionist Clifton Chenier. I'd laugh as he tried to show me how to do the James Brown. Mick glided effortlessly across the living room floor, but I couldn't get the hang of it.

Patti Boyd invited Mick and me up to Friar Park, where she and George lived in an amazing fortress in Henley-on-Thames. Usually Mick's chauffeur, Alan, drove us around in the white Bentley, but today it was just the two of us, off to Oxfordshire with the top down. While Mick drove I played Motown 45s on his state-of-the-art portable record player, secured under the glove box. As we neared the castle, I could see the Union Jack flying along with a skull and cross-bones from the uppermost turret of George's estate. Hare Krishna devotees were plowing and seeding a rural plot on George's thirty-five-acre estate. There were breathtaking Victorian gardens surrounded by miles of whimsical man-made lakes that Mick, Patti, George, and I later boated around in. There were also mysterious underground caverns that made it feel like a Victorian Disneyland.

The Gothic mansion had previously been a convent, and the former nuns had filled in all of the lakes with earth. George said that when he bought the place he'd had the same contractor who had filled them in return and dig them all out again. While Mick and George had tea in the kitchen, Patti took me on the grand tour. There were at least five stories, and more then a hundred rooms. The Hare Krishnas lived on the high top floor, but the mansion was so immense you'd never know a soul was there.

Every room was like a palace, with religious stained glass, Victorian painted murals, inlaid floors, and molded seraphs swooping down from the corners of the ceilings. I was amused to see that the sisters had also painted loincloths on every cherub in the manor. As George and Patti had only recently acquired this enormous fortress, except for an Eastern religious shrine with an ancient Buddha and fresh-cut flowers, there was little in the way of furnishings. Most of our day was spent in the big, cozy rectory-like kitchen.

I was having an amazing, dreamy time with Mick Jagger, and we were becoming an item. Envious girls would whisper, "Do you think she really loves him?"

What was not to love? He was painfully beautiful, sweetly romantic. He had amazing taste, sophistication, and was some kind of lover. Yes, I was crazy about him. At twenty years old, who wouldn't be?

It was late August 1970, and the Stones were about to go do a European tour. Mick thought it would be nice if we took a little holiday to Paris before his departure. Heather and Roger Daltrey took Damian off to Berkshire, and I flew across the channel with Mick for a romantic weekend in Paris.

We stayed at Johnny Hallyday's, the French Elvis Presley's country home, nestled in the forest of Honfleur, just outside Deauville. In the afternoons we took long walks in the secluded backwoods and hunted for truffles. In the evening, the guests of the house would sit at an extended candlelit table, where stunning food that had simmered all afternoon arrived in several courses throughout the evening. The final course was fresh peaches and stinky cheese. The aged cheese smelled like sweaty old socks but tasted like lifetimes. It was luscious with the crusted French bread and vintage ruby merlot. The French guests dipped slices of fresh peach into their wine glasses and savored it from the points of their knives. Being with Mick, the warm candlelight, and sensuous French accents, the sound of clinking glasses and laughter, all had a dreamy elegance, which has stayed in my head like indelible photographs.

Back at Heathrow Airport, and being a Yankee, I had to go through special customs, and once again the customs agent denied me entry. My visa had expired, and he wasn't letting me back into the United Kingdom. I didn't think he'd actually believe my story, but I gave it a go: "I'm on holiday with Mick Jagger, he's just gone to pick up our luggage."

My declaration only made it worse; besides being an illegal, he now assumed I was a mental case. "Please come with me, madam."

Mick finally came to the rescue, and I may as well have been with the pope. The customs agent got Mick's autograph, and I was granted a full year extension on my visa.

Early the next morning Mick was off to Brussels for the Stones' European tour. I was half asleep when he kissed me good-bye, promising to call when he got to Brussels. He was wearing the black-and-white houndstooth trousers, the ones he'd worn when I first met him, and it made me smile. I was faintly awake long enough to see him disappear through the bedroom door.

I didn't know it then, but this was to be our last kiss, our last moment. Our sweet time was up; I would never see Mick again.

We talked on the phone and made plans for after the tour, which would only be a month away. I still had a plane ticket to California, and felt secure enough to go back for a visit while he was away. After the tour we planned to meet in Los Angeles, or I'd fly back to London. I closed up the house on Cheyne Walk, and left a black-and-white photo-booth picture of myself with a smoochy soft lip print on the back. I then boarded the train at Victoria Station and was on my way to Berkshire to collect my son and have a visit with the lovely Heather. Roger was on tour with the Who, and Heather was happy to have a bit of company.

The three of us ate like it was the Last Supper. Every day we'd trot down to the local village in full mod, hippie regalia, with young Damian, three dogs, and a rolling shopping basket in tow. We'd stop at the local bakery and procure still-warm-from-the-oven country bread, then slather it with creamy English butter. Heather showed me how to make the most delicious apple pie, using the tart apples from her tree in the garden.

We got a surprise call from London; it was Devon Wilson, Heather's friend and comrade from New York. Devon was a pretty black girl with a New York street edge, acerbic tongue, and dark, funny sense of humor. She was with Jimi Hendrix, and they wanted to come up for the weekend. Heather and I had no idea what was in store.

Jimi and Devon arrived in a minicab, along with a couple of friends. It was a lovely September afternoon, and we all enjoyed a nice, civilized cup of tea in the garden. Jimi loved Roger and Heather's cottage, and the tranquillity of Berkshire. As outrageous as Jimi appeared, he was actually quite shy and soft-spoken. He had a gracious, gentle nature, and always made you feel special. He said he wished he had a home of his own, that he was tired of living in hotels. In essence, he was a homeless, wandering gypsy, but he really wanted to settle down, and maybe even get married.

Devon had brought along some LSD, and without a thought we all downed it with our afternoon tea. By nightfall we were howling at the moon, accompanied by Neil Young's new album, *After the Gold Rush*, and Bob Dylan's *Bringing It All Back Home* on the stereo. Out of the blue, Jimi's friends said they had to get back to London, and called a minicab to take them home, leaving the four of us as high as psychedelic kites. Jimi and Devon were recounting Dylan lyrics in the living room, then Jimi went off on his own mystical riff. The most profound, transcendent poetry began flowing effortlessly from his lips. It was as if it was being channeled from beyond, and his words were all in amazing flawless rhyme. As he spoke I could see sparkling diamonds, rubies, and sapphires falling from his lips. Heather and I were both in awe. We agreed we should be recording Jimi, or at least writing it down. Unfortunately we were way too high to do anything but listen in reverence.

I think Devon and Jimi had taken something besides the acid. Devon was staggering around, so completely out of it that Heather had to help her upstairs and put her to bed.

Jimi could barely stand, and repeatedly asked, "Do you have any more Mandies, or some Valium?"

I had already given Jimi two Mandrax, but he had already forgot he'd even taken them. He was now stumbling and toppling into us and the furniture like an unsteady drunkard. Despite his tipsy state, he was still enchantingly charming, until he finally passed out cold on the floor. Heather and I were going to just cover him with a blanket, but then decided we didn't want young Damian to come down in the morning and find Jimi comatose on the living room carpet. Heather took his arms, I grabbed his legs, and we lugged Jimi Hendrix up the narrow wooden staircase. He was a ton of dead weight, and it took us twenty minutes of huffing, puffing, and careful maneuvering to get sweet Mr. Jimi to bed. We'd seen Jimi pretty high in the past, but never like this. We went down to the kitchen and put the kettle on for a calming cup of tea. Heather sighed. "Oh God, what if he ODs here? Roger will kill me."

"Let's go check, make sure he's breathing," I said.

Just then, Jimi appeared like a shadow in the doorway, saying, "I'm here for the interview."

Five days later, on September 18, we got a call from London; our dear Mr. Jimi had departed permanently.

Soon after that, with my two-year-old son in tow, I boarded British Airways for what I thought was going to be a short visit to California. I stayed with Mimi, who was now in her early sixties but still staggeringly youthful, not a line or wrinkle in her beautiful cream-puff face. Phone calls from Mick became less frequent, and soon came to a deafening halt. The next thing I knew Mick was all over the covers of every tabloid in Los Angeles with a new girl, the exotic Bianca, by his side. To be sure, I called his house in Chelsea and an austere-sounding woman with an imported accent answered, inquiring, "Ooo is thees?"

My heart went thud; I could picture her all propped up and cozy on my side of the bed. In a split second the romantic summer I'd spent with Mick flashed through my head, and I gently put the phone down on the receiver.

11

'd certainly got my fill of sex, drugs, and rock and roll. In my heart of hearts all I truly ever wanted was a somewhat sane family of my own, and maybe a little house in the country, but simplicity always seemed to elude me. I'd had this idea that somewhere in the universe there was a country girl who longed for the city lights. I was the city girl who longed for the heartland; it was simply a cosmic mix-up. I had a son now, and this was my chance. I could give him the life I'd dreamed of.

With the five hundred pounds I got from signing off on the Air Force album, I took my son and headed east from Los Angeles. Maybe I'd find a place in Woodstock, in upstate New York.

From our modest motel room in the rural village of Brewster, New York, I pored over the rental listings in the local *Gazette*. I found an ad that read, "Log cabin on lake in Connecticut. Two hundred dollars a month, call Perry Katz."

In my rental car I followed Perry's directions along the lakeside until the road ended and became unpaved gravel. Old Mr. Katz was parked out front in a spanking new white Caddy convertible. He sported a fancy white yachting cap, and was smoking a chubby cigar— not at all like I'd pictured him.

The enchanting old cabin was built of smooth, peeled cherry logs and sat on a grassy knoll overlooking Candlewood Lake. It was the beginning of October, and in the final days of a late Indian summer. The sun was softly pale and the air had the crisp chill of impending winter. The only sound to be heard was a light wind blowing through the tall surrounding Noble pines. Inside, the cabin was dark, and had the musty smell of a freshly opened, vintage trunk. Perry explained that the old place hadn't been lived in for many years. His stately summerhouse was at the other side of the lake; he only used this stead to store his old furniture, which I was welcome to use.

When he opened the dusty plank storm shutters, the cottage filled with light. The living room had a twenty-foot ceiling with heavy crossbeams and a log staircase that led up to a cozy little loft. The whole place had a peaceful tranquillity, a calmness that reminded me of Heidi's cabin in the Alps. There was a huge granite fireplace that reached the rafters and wide floorboards of smooth pine. The surrounding porch was screened in, and paned windows opened out to a view of the pristine lake. I was home; this would be the perfect place to raise my blond three-year-old cherub.

Before signing the lease Perry asked in a hushed voice, "You don't have any jungle bunny friends, do you?"

I'd never heard that expression before, and didn't have a clue what he was talking about. He said, "You know, spear chuckers."

I didn't know a soul in Connecticut, and now I was really confused. I imagined Watusi warriors leaping from the bushes, heaving spears.

"No rabbits," I piped. "Just a pair of singing canaries."

Our first winter in Connecticut was the coldest the East Coast had experienced in fifteen years. The gale blowing off the frozen lake made it a chilling fifteen below zero. Ten-foot pointy icicles hung from my shingled eaves like frozen fringe, and solid snowdrifts blocked the doors from opening. I hadn't noticed before, but some of the logs had spaces where the sealant had cracked, and the icy wind came howling through. It was a bona fide winter wonderland.

While my landlord was wintering in Florida, yachting around the keys, my son and I were snowbound at the North Pole. I didn't know when I rented the place, but this was basically a summerhouse, a rural vacation spot where New Yorkers came up for the summertime holiday. We may as well have been holed up in the far corners of Siberia, as there wasn't a soul to be seen for miles. Still, I wasn't deterred; I simply caulked the cracks with Fixall and stapled sheets of clear plastic on the outside of the windows.

There were all sorts of wonderful treasures in the attic. I dragged out an old chest stuffed with patchwork quilts from the 1800s, an old Mission dresser, and an oak Stickley bench, which I've lugged into the present. There was an ornate iron bed for Damian, and a huge pirate's trunk to store his toys in. The heavy mattresses were stuffed with horsehair, which Perry insisted was the finest of stuffing.

Just when I thought I was getting the hang of winter, Fairfield County was besieged by yet another blizzard. After a freezing ice storm, the pines, brush, everything around, all looked as if they'd been dipped in a fragile coat of glistening glass. The wind howled like the moors of Wuthering Heights, and all of a sudden the power along with the furnace conked out, leaving us without heat and in silent darkness. I remembered a mound of stacked wood out in the back, and proceeded to build my best Girl Scout–style fire. At first the blaze caught so well the flames started lapping the Christmas cards right off the granite mantel top, then the cabin began to fill with dense, stifling smoke. I ran and doused the flames with pots of water and had to rip down my makeshift plastic storm windows before I could get the windows open to let the smoke out.

There we were, my little son and I, in the pitch dark. We were in middle of nowhere in a raging blizzard with the windows wide open and flapping in the wind.

I soon learned how to open the flue cover and became an expert at wielding an ax. If the wood was damp, instead of blowing the flames and myself into hyperventilation, I'd reverse the hose on the vintage Electrolux vacuum and stoke the kindling into glowing embers. It had taken twenty years, but I had finally gotten my dream: I had my three-year-old baby, and I was becoming quite the country girl. The only problem was, I was also next to penniless.

Out of a newspaper ad I found a babysitter and got myself a position as a cash register girl at the local Caldor chain store. Caldor was roughly two miles into town, and each morning I'd maneuver the wet, slippery snow in my Corky platform sandals, wearing them with kneesocks to keep my legs warm. The concept of real winter clothes hadn't yet occurred to me. When I discovered a simple pair of fur-lined gloves would keep my chapped hands from freezing off, it felt like Christmas.

The free Connecticut *PennySaver* paper was my salvation and lifeline to the outside world, and living in the woods, I definitely needed a car. I found a Volkswagen that looked pretty good for $150. The sellers were quite friendly and definitely had themselves a live one with an inexperienced California girl. I wasn't yet savvy enough to check for things like rusting erosion from the salted roads, or if the heater even worked. All I knew was that the bug started up okay, and the radio sounded good. I paid my 150 big ones, and was on my merry way back to Pocono Point, when I must have struck a slushy pothole. Out of the dark night heavens, it felt as if someone had tossed a brimming bucket of icy cold water straight into my face. The frigid road water had splashed up from the floorboard and completely drenched me. By the time I got home, my long locks were literally frozen stiff. I lifted up the floor mat and found a gaping hole the size of a crater; I could see clear to the gravel on the ground. The entire floorboard was rusted out, and the sellers had hidden the damage with a flimsy rubber mat. I'd been had.

With a babe in arms and zero cash to spare, I was desperate for dependable transportation. I placed a simple ad in the *PennySaver:* WANTED: FREE CAR. I got several responses and chose the person with the Pontiac, because he lived in the nearest town and the car had an automatic transmission. I hired a taxi that took us the ten miles to New Milford, and there was my new car, sitting out in an open field. It was a silver bomb, the size of a boat, but in amazingly great shape. My good Samaritan, Mr. Forrester, was a nice-looking gent who appeared to be in his late thirties. He said he'd planned to donate the car and was happy I could have it. He seemed almost apologetic that some of the silver paint on the hood had lost its luster, but pointed out the new tires and the well-kept pearly gray leather interior.

When I had placed the ad, I fully expected to get a car, but now that I was actually here I could barely believe my good fortune. This was an amazing car, fully loaded with power steering, seats, windows, the lot! When I put the headlights on, a glowing silhouette of the Pontiac Indian head lit up on the dash in blue. As he signed the pink slip over and handed me the keys, I felt almost humbled. This was my very first car of my own. All I could think to say was, "Thank you very much, I don't have words to express how much I appreciate this."

Driving off felt a little strange, but with a touch of merriment, I said an out loud thank you to God, then looked over at my son on the cushy leather bench seat.

"Ask and you shall receive," I said.

Working at Caldor department store wasn't exactly a financial windfall, and it was incredibly dreary. After taxes the babysitter's cut was more then I was earning. I also didn't like being away from my son eight hours of his waking day. I needed an occupation that would allow me to bring my little boy along. I found another ad in the *PennySaver* that read: "Make three hundred dollars a week in your spare time, call Bob." Bingo! That was for me.

The guy on the phone had a somber-sounding diction, like he was alone in a dismal, dimly lit room, but I decided to let him come to my house and give me the power pitch.

Mr. Bob was as mysterious as I'd imagined. He was an older man in his sixties, neatly dressed in a well-cared-for, dated brown suit and for-ties tie. His felt-brimmed fedora made him look like Philip Marlowe, fresh from an Alcoholics Anonymous meeting. It turned out he was the Fuller Brush Man. Not exactly what I had in mind, but I was close to bankrupt and decided to give it a go. He gave me a stack of order sheets and Fuller Brush catalogs, and I was ready to conquer Fairfield County.

Not yet twenty-one, I'd gone from living with Mick Jagger to door-to-door broom sales, and was actually doing quite well. I drove the Pontiac with little Damian by my side and canvassed the historic neighborhoods of Ridgefield. The first week I sold five hundred dol-lars' worth of mops, brooms, and boar-bristle hairbrushes. Nothing compares to the feeling of knocking on strangers' doors trying to in-terest them in a mop.

I was all excited to get my first check, which turned out to be a lofty fifty dollars. Fifty dollars, how could that be?

Mr. Bob said, "Yes, ma'am, that would be ten percent of five hundred."

Hmm, back to the *PennySaver*.

Next I found old Mrs. Wheeler, a Southern matriarch whose black cook, Olive Hercules, had died after forty-five years of service. In her Southern drawl she said she could tell by my voice that I wasn't colored, but to come over anyway and they'd take a look at me.

Mr. and Mrs. Wheeler were lovely old racists who lived in a colonial mansion on a horse farm in ritzy Ridgefield, Connecticut. Their land was so extensive the street was named Wheeler Road. The Wheelers took an instant liking to me, and to my cherub, and hired me on the spot. As Mrs. Wheeler showed me around the mansion, she pointed out the two bathrooms on the parlor floor.

"This one is for the servants," she whispered. With her hand hushed to her lips, she said, "But we'd like you to use our bathroom."

Over my twenty years on the planet I'd heard about racism but never experienced it firsthand. I felt strange agreeing to something so absurd, but went along with her archaic custom and used the appointed facilities.

Besides myself, there were Alice and Franklin, the Wheelers' long-faithful black maid and trusted butler. Both wore crisp uniforms, and Franklin even wore white gloves while he served the meals I prepared.

I was a pretty good cook, but certainly not a professional chef. At the Wheelers' home, everything had to be made fresh and from scratch. Alice picked apples from the tree in the garden, and I used Heather Daltrey's fail-proof recipe for apple pie. Each morning the Missus would submit a menu, which included fresh grilled chicken or braised beef for Binky, their pampered miniature pooch.

Today the lunch entrée would be the Southern lamb pie topped with warm buttermilk biscuits. The only biscuits I knew how to bake came from Pillsbury, packaged in a blue-rolled container. I panicked and started searching the pantry for a fragment of a cookbook. On the top shelf in the very back I found a dusty old recipe volume. For a brief moment I was relieved, until I realized that the edition was from

1892. Baking soda, yeast, lard? I didn't have a clue. My biscuits came fresh out of the oven with the consistency of toasted dirt clumps, which Franklin delivered in an ornate sterling silver dish. Soon after dinner was served, the antiquated electric bell system summoned me from the kitchen. Mrs. Wheeler wanted to see me. She complimented me on my lamb "pah," and kindly mentioned that the biscuits were a little hard. Sadly, the lumps in my Southern chicken pan gravy were not much softer.

As it turned out, it wasn't my cooking that endeared me to the Wheelers. They delighted in having Damian and me for a bit of company. Edward Wheeler loved tooling around on his tractor with young Master Damian perched on his lap. They'd ride up to the stables to feed carrots and sugar cubes to the horses. Miss Elenore was getting too old and frail to handle the big Lincoln in the garage and enjoyed having me drive her to the shops in the village. I was used to speeding around in the cushy Pontiac, but in the Lincoln, and before seatbelts, just a tap on the power brakes caused her fragile, light body to surge off the seat. I'd put my arm out across her chest like Mimi used to do when I was little, and push her back in the soft bench seat.

There was a mysterious little two-story residence on the far end of the Wheelers' property that Elenore wanted to visit.

The cottage looked like a place in heaven. There was an inviting pair of Adirondack chairs flanking the entrance, and it was surrounded by a lovely garden afresh with wildflowers and newly blooming narcissus. The main room was a wide-open space with a comfy cabbage rose–covered sofa. In the corner sat an impressive grand piano laden with framed photos of a pretty dark-haired young woman. There were trophies, blue ribbons, and pictures of horses everywhere. It was a Ralph Lauren paradise with the odd, still feeling of a ghost town. The upstairs bedroom was full of light, with a four-poster bed, slanted ceiling, and dotted violet wallpaper. It was all just heavenly. Elenore told me this house had been her daughter Jennifer's home. She'd been killed in a horse-riding accident twenty years ago, at the age of twenty-one. I was the same age. Elenore and Edward had talked it over, and wanted Damian and me to come and live in the cottage, be part of their family.

This was all too amazing to be true. I could have the sweet parents I'd always dreamed of, and in return they'd have a daughter and the grandchild they'd dreamed of. It was a life-changing decision, like God was offering me an alternative, an easier path. I'd always thought that before I was born I was given the choice of a temperate life experience or a crash course, so I could get it all in one go. I had chosen the crash course, and always held steady on course. For some reason I wasn't ready to give up the struggle; I was just getting started. I thrived on the challenge and loved my own little paradise on Candlewood Lake. I declined their generous offer, and they eventually employed a more experienced sauce chef and buttermilk biscuit baker.

Summer was nearing, and the ninety-mile lake had almost thawed. It had been one adventurous winter.

There were times when I couldn't afford oil for the furnace, and it got so cold my son and I could see our breath in the frosty air. My canaries gave birth to three tiny delicate, dotted-blue eggs. When they hatched I'd tried to keep their featherless pink bodies warm with a lightbulb close to their nest, but they didn't survive the cold and died one after the next. I could have asked Mimi for help with the heating oil, but I was proud, I wanted to be independent, and I didn't want her to worry about us.

Late in the night I often heard what sounded like an assembly up in the attic. Directly above my bed there were thumps, dragging sounds, and bed-frame coils rebounding. There was also a medley of rummaging sounds in the distance. My heart pounded like a sledgehammer as I listened, trying to decipher sounds in the dark. It turned out to be a family of raccoons, some sprightly mice nesting in the attic, and a few stray opossums shaking down the garbage cans, but I still felt uneasy. I was alone with a child, there were no neighbors, and the nights were as dark as pitch. Being alone in the woods with a child, I felt vulnerable. In case there were any real intruders, I mapped out an escape route. My simple plan was to gather my tot, scramble out the back, and wait by the pier on the lake till the coast was clear. Every jittery night I'd deliberate, should we move closer to town? My heart couldn't take much more distress. When the sun finally rose, the lake and all its surroundings were so radiant, I'd reconsider and stay put.

One starless night all my imaginative visions were about to become a real-life drama. I heard a car in the distance, its horn blasting, barreling down my private, unpaved road. I kept the lights out and peeked out the curtain long enough to see a dark, four-door sedan turn around and career up my lawn, almost crashing into my stone steps. When the passenger door opened the interior light came on, illuminating four threatening-looking young brawlers. As they neared my door I was sure I would go into cardiac arrest. No time for my rehearsed escape plan. Instead I ran to the phone and called the sheriff. By now they were throwing rocks at the house, and one of them was banging on my front door shouting, "Open up!"

My front door was pretty sturdy, with a wide wooden plank that slid vertically across and fit into a log casing.

Now the intruders were trying to kick the door in, and the wood was beginning to splinter. I bravely yelled out, "You guys better go. I've called the police!"

The male on the other side growled,

"If anyone's called the police, it's gonna be for murder!"

Hearing that, I just about died on the spot.

The other three were in the distance, swigging from liquor bottles and howling like a tribe of drunken banshees. All I could think of was

My handsome dad decked out in his racing gear.

My dad posing on his motorcycle in his high heels.

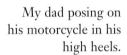

My dad as Robin in full female glory.

My young dad in his Black Foxe military uniform.

My young dad with Busby Berkeley in front of Ozeta Terrace.

My father posing in front of his Cadillac and holding an ever present bottle of brew.

Me and my grandfather Al with the missing fingers. This picture was taken on the back lot of MGM Studios.

My beautiful grandmother Mimi in the 1920s.

My breathtaking Mimi with her two beautiful daughters, my mother and her older sister Joanne.

My mother, Diana Dearest.

My dramatic young mother at age twenty.

My mother dressed as a geisha for Halloween. She made this costume and did her own hair and makeup.

Me in Central Park six months after I ran away
from California. I was just fifteen trying to look
twenty. *Photograph by David Hoff*

Denny Laine in front of our freezing country house in England.

Denny dressing up for the night.

Me at age nineteen grooming my two-year-old cherub after his bath.

Me and Damian boating on the lake with Jackson in Echo Park. *Photo by Jackson Browne*

My son, Damian, at age three.

My family: Damian showing off his new red tire pump and our cat Morgan by my side at our cottage in Connecticut.

Our backyard in Connecticut after a first snow.

In the photo booth at the train station on one of our many trips to New York City.

VANESSA

Height 5'8"
Dress 5-7-8
Bust 33
Waist 23
Hips 33
Shoe 7½
Glove 7
Hat 22¾
Hair Brunette
Eyes Green

EXCELLENT LEGS

Wilhelmina
9 EAST 37 STREET
NEW YORK CITY 10016

PRINT: 532-6806
TV: 889-9450

Christa Modeling
9 Rue Keppler
Paris 16
720.4100
Telex Chromod 61972 F

My Wilhelmina modeling card. *Photograph by Sal Carbo*

One of my glamorous head shots; I'm twenty-three here.
Photograph by Gary Gross

One of my first test shots in a bathing suit. *Photograph © Richard Selby*

Me at twenty-six in a ballerina modeling photo. *Photograph © Suzanne Nyerges*

Me and my dog Molly by the lakefront in Connecticut.

My beautiful aunt Claire in a studio publicity shot.

My sweet cousin Blake on the veranda of Ozeta Terrace.

My boyfriend Paul Zacha at his wildly artistic desk at Center Studios in Hollywood.

Me standing in for Diane Keaton with the director of photography, Dante Spinotti, during the filming of *The Other Sister*.

Me photo doubling for Diane Keaton in the film *Town and Country*.

Patti D'Arbanville and me on the set of *New York Undercover*.

Me digging through one of the Dumpsters at my deceased father's house in Palm Springs. *Photograph © Ovid Pope*

After a Sunday lunch in Greenwich Village, in 1995. Left to right: Roger Daltrey, me, Dave, Andrea, an unknown friend, and the lovely Heather, Roger's wife.

My friends Michael and Pamela Des Barres at a Halloween party.

Roger and me, in 2006.

Me and my teen grandson John.
Photograph © Lisa Law

My son, Damian, all grown up.

my innocent little son, who was miraculously still sleeping upstairs in the loft. I tried to reason with them saying, "There's only one road out; the police are going to get you."

Thankfully, I heard one of them say, "Come on, man, forget it, let's go."

But the buck at the door spewed, "I'm going in."

I was never more scared in all my life. I grabbed the ax that I split the logs with, ready to do battle; at least I'd have the first blow.

I was suited up, ready to take my best shot, when I saw the flashing red lights of a squad car descending down my street. My rowdy road warriors tried to make a run for it, but as I had warned them, there was nowhere to run. The four of them were quickly arrested and sent to the local lockup.

If I was going to continue living in the forest, I definitely needed some sort of security plan. A pistol was the obvious choice, but the mere sight of a gun had always made me feel woozy. If I'd had a gun would I have shot one of those guys?

What I needed was a decoy, I reasoned. A few more cars would help so I didn't look like a lone sitting duck. I still had the Volkswagen with the missing floorboards and the luxurious Pontiac. My next procurement was a Humber Super Snipe, courtesy of the *PennySaver*. The Super Snipe was an English postwar steel-gray tanker with the posh interior of a Bentley. The seats were soft gray leather with a burled rosewood dashboard. There were even quaint fold-down rosewood trays that flipped out on the back of the seats. My last, and favorite, car was a 1960 British racing green MGA convertible, which inevitably needed a push to get it started. Each day I'd rotate the order of the cars, like people were coming and going, and drive them around the lake to keep the batteries charged. The Pontiac was the most reliable and the best fun.

Near our house were two steep dips in the road. I found that if I got up enough speed on the straightaway, the car would become airborne, then softly land on the descent. When we'd get to that spot my four-year-old would urge me on, "Make the car fly, Mom!"

It was our little amusement. I'm not sure which one of us liked it more.

Toward the end of May, near Memorial Day, I found I actually had neighbors. The city people began to arrive, breathing life back into the handful of seemingly abandoned cottages dotting the shoreline. They were mostly families with kids, and a few older retired couples. My serene, unruffled lake was now jumping with sail- and motorboats, fishing vacationers luxuriating in water-skiing and barbecuing tasty-smelling burgers. It was a whole new summer movie, and me and my son were the talk of the block. I was the eccentric girl on the lake, the girl from Hollywood with an angelic four-year-old. At the communal lakefront I'd chitchat with the middle-aged housewives, who looked at me with suspicious, raised brows. A few of the husbands were a bit friendlier, and sometimes showed up at my cottage door like old stray dogs. I often awoke to find a stringer laden with slippery perch and whiskered catfish flopping around, gasping for breath on my screened-in porch. Damian and I would free the catch, removing the cordage from their gills and gullets; then we'd place the fish in the bathtub full of water and try to revive the poor sods. Half the fish would turn on their sides from the lack of oxygen, but if we kept pushing them around upright, they usually made a comeback, making our bathtub look like a thriving fishpond. Not wanting to appear ungracious for the humble offerings, I'd wait till dusk, then load up the live cargo into deep roasting pans full of water. We would carefully slide the pans into the backseat of the vintage Humber and shuttle the fish to the other side of the lake to set them free. Damian and I spent half the summer transporting the slimy catches back to the lakeside. It was our secret undercover operation.

The balmy summer made the uncertain, frigid winter well worth the price of admission. When the lake began to thaw and the first crocus bloomed, I remembered why I had fallen in love with this place.

Besides being shatteringly beautiful, Connecticut had a profusion of unmined antiques and unknown treasures. I haunted country barn auctions, and church and tag sales, and started my collection of antique pre-Raphaelite and Maxfield Parrish prints. I bought up every Victorian embroidered shawl and patchwork quilt I could find, and started a little enterprise selling them in New York for triple the money. Damian and I skated at the town roller rink, and watched movies at the drive-in theater, and my little boy learned how to swim in the clear waters of Candlewood. Whatever there was to do, we did it. I planted a garden of wildflowers and a variety of organic vegetables; started a freshwater aquarium for Damian; and adopted a regal Russian wolfhound from an ad in the *PennySaver*. As lovely as it all was, I was feeling a bit lonely. After reading my son to sleep I'd turn up Puccini and gaze out over the moonlit water, thinking how romantic it was here. Where was my handsome young prince? If he even existed, I certainly wasn't making it easy for him to find me.

Out of the blue I got a call from Jackson Browne. We'd written and spoken on the phone a few times, but I hadn't seen him since he saw me off at British Airways, the day I left him standing at the gate to go and be with Denny Laine in England. Jackson had just finished his first album and was in New York to promote it. He said that since he was so close to Connecticut, he'd like to come up for a visit.

Damian and I were waiting on the country-style platform as his train rolled into Brewster station. Jackson was hanging off the edge of the old-fashioned caboose, holding out a copy of *Saturate Before Using*, his first record. My sweet Jackson, he did it! As we embraced, memories of our past romance flooded through my head like it was yesterday.

The touch and smell of him still sent me. After a cozy home-cooked dinner, I asked if he'd like to stay the night. He looked at me with his soulful brown eyes, and sighed. "No, I can't. I have to get back to L.A."

The possibility that he'd decline my invitation hadn't even occurred to me. I asked why, and he told me about his new girlfriend in Los Angeles. He said he was in love with her. I got an ill feeling in my belly, probably like what he must have felt when I ran off to England. I put on my best pretend smile, and graciously wished him well.

Was this it? Would I be alone for eternity, and never have sex again? Oh, well. I'd never really triumphed in romance, but I was raising a healthy child, and we lived in paradise. I was becoming comfortable with my solitary fate, and was actually having the best time in my life when I got an unexpected call from Jimmy Page.

No matter how much time went by, the sound of Jimmy's soft, reticent voice always stopped my heart cold. I hadn't seen him in over two years, but his voice still made my insides stir. He was in New York at the Drake Hotel, and asked if he could come up for the weekend. I thought, "This has to be a dream."

Jimmy's glistening black limousine looked so out of place on my sylvan country road, and my summer neighbors were even more bewildered.

Jimmy was just as dazzling as the last time we met. He's also the only man who has ever left me at a loss for words. I don't know why, but I always felt slightly shy with him. I was more mature now, a whole twenty-one years. I thought I was a bit more self-assured, but the mere sight of him getting out of his limo and strolling up my walk gave me the familiar jitters. Trying to maintain some sense of coolness, I greeted Jimmy like he was a distant cousin. With a quick kiss, I announced, "Damian and I are just off to the market; you're welcome to wait here or come along if you like."

He said he wanted to go with us, and I showed him how I made the silver Pontiac fly over the dips in the road. We were having a sweet time, and my coolness quickly turned into mush. We had a late-night candlelit dinner and kissed till our lips were swollen to Joni Mitchell's *Court and Spark* album. Jimmy and I passed the weekend in the summer glory of Candlewood Lake. I took him on a tour of my rural terrain and antique haunts. We took splendid late-afternoon walks with my son and Molly, our Russian wolfhound. It was everything I'd imagined. A noble young man had indeed found the path to my door, and I was back in the dreamy days of Avalon.

Jimmy finally said the magic words: "Why don't you come to England?"

Any other time I would have gone like an arrow, but now I'd started a life, I had a son, birds, fish, a dog, and a flourishing vegetable garden to look after. I couldn't just leave everything and run off to England, but I did accept his invitation to go with him to Los Angeles for a Led Zeppelin show at the Shrine.

I bribed a girlfriend from New York with an all-expense-paid week in Candlewood paradise to look after my son, and Jimmy and I boarded a jet to Los Angeles.

Neither of us was crazy about flying, but the in-flight movie was a welcome distraction. The movie was *Brian's Song*, the tragic story of football player Brian Piccolo's untimely demise. By the time James Caan was on his deathbed, Jimmy and I were rolling with laughter in first class, clearly offending the other teary-eyed passengers.

A Mercedes limo was waiting at LAX to whisk us off to the Continental Riot (Hyatt) House, Zeppelin's notorious quarters on Sunset Strip. The word was out—Zeppelin was in town. The lobby was a-flurry with pretty young girls ready and waiting to show their wares, desirous for a chance to pay homage to their English idols.

The shows at the Shrine were stunning. The silhouette of Jimmy cloaked in shimmery velvet, moons and stars, and the haunting, abandoned sound of the bow gliding across his guitar were enchantingly sensual. To me Jimmy was Led Zeppelin, the sorcerer behind the magic; he definitely had it down.

After my whirlwind week of rock and steamy, romantic sex, I actually looked forward to the sanctuary of my little house, away from the glitz and glamour of Hollywood. The beauty of Connecticut in 1971 made Los Angeles feel like a worn-out high heel.

The Indian summer was waning, and the city vacationers had packed up their boats and barbecues and scooted back to New York City. This was my favorite time of the year. The pale changing light and cool quiescent lake softly lapped the bank and flocks of migrating Canadian geese landed on my shore for a brief repose. Sometimes there were so many plaintive honkers Damian and I would get scared and hightail it back to the safety of the cottage.

On my narrow road the trees grew together like a glorious covered bridge. Just before the leaves fell, they'd burst into the most luminous shades of pinks, yellows, and reds I'd ever seen. I never missed a day to absorb the beauty. It was our own heavenly little Walden Pond, and we loved it there.

Although Lake Candlewood seemed a million miles from civilization, it was really only two hours by train from the bustle of New York City. I got a letter from Denny, who said he was coming to New York in December, along with Paul McCartney and their new band, Wings. He asked if he could come up to Connecticut to spend some time with our son. After our last encounter I wasn't sure this was such a great idea. I was well over my drama with Denny and his turbulent behavior, but on the other hand I thought it would be good for our five-year-old son to spend some time with his father. Damian and I picked Denny up from the Brewster station. Seeing Denny on American soil felt strangely out of context. He also looked completely different. He'd cut his sixties-style long hair into a Caesar-style do and sported a small gold ring in his newly pierced ear.

In the beginning it was actually nice to see Denny again. One admirable thing about him was that he was quite generous when he could afford to be. He took Damian shopping for winter clothes and filled my kitchen cupboards with all the amenities and nice things I'd been unable to afford. He got a laugh out of my car collection, but thought I needed something a little spiffier. We searched the ads in the *PennySaver* and found a promising little Mini Cooper just like the one Denny drove in England. The car was fifty miles to God knows where in the outskirts of Connecticut, and Denny bought me the Mini on the spot. I now had the Pontiac, the Volkswagen, the Humber, the 1962 MGA convertible I had picked up for fifty dollars, plus the Mini. A total of five decoy automobiles were parked in my front garden.

I built crackling fires with the cord of wood Denny had delivered, and the three of us danced around the log cabin like delighted children to T.Rex's "Bang a Gong." There was no romance, but things were going swimmingly well until Denny took the liberty to tell me, "If you come back to England, I'll give you whatever you want."

I was briefly almost interested, until he followed it up with, "But if you don't, you'll get nothing from me."

There's something about an ultimatum that never sat well with me. I was the sort of girl who would rather take her chances backpacking in a minefield than abide stipulations. In my willful stance I declared, "I'll take nothing then."

From there on in, it was the downhill slope. The serene country air was dense with old, familiar bitterness. I had that same sick feeling in my stomach that I used to get when we lived together in England. I just wanted him to go away before things got out of hand.

The snow was falling like the heavens had opened, and the fire had burned down to a flickering ember. I asked Denny if he would go out in the back and get some more logs to stoke up the fire. I still can't imagine where I found the impetus to be so wicked, but as soon as he walked out the door, I locked it behind him, leaving him standing in the falling snow.

As he knocked, pounded, and pleaded at the back door for me to let him back in, I grabbed his coat and bags and set them out on the front porch. I held my ground till he finally gave up and trudged the six miles through the powdery snow back to the train station. It would be some twenty years before Damian would see his father again.

With all my endeavors, paying the bills was still a struggle. Denny had been sending me £100 a month, roughly $125, but now I wouldn't be getting a shilling. I'd only had a few years of formal education, and I didn't want to take work that kept me away from raising my boy. It was a particularly frosty winter and the heating oil was burning fast. I didn't have the seventy-five dollars to refill the oil tank, and Damian and I were close to freezing. We slept together under my electric blanket in my king-sized bed, and during the day we stayed close to the fire. There had to be a better way.

It was 1973 when it occurred to me that I could possibly make some money modeling in the city. I dug out some old Polaroids of myself and made an appointment at the renowned Wilhelmina modeling agency.

At the reception desk I encountered the mighty Kay. Kay was Wilhelmina's shrewd screener and main booker of the models. Getting past her was just the first hurdle. She took a quick, aloof glance at my snapshots, then asked me to wait in the reception. After what seemed like an hour of watching sultry young models saunter in and out of the office, Kay ushered me in to see the chief. The radiant Wilhelmina had been a model in the early sixties and looked like a pristine page out of a Richard Avedon book. She was dressed in an impeccably tailored black suit and a crisp white shirt, buttoned to the neck. Her smooth auburn hair was pulled back tight into a perfect chignon. Sitting across from her grand lectern in the adjacent smaller chair was painfully intimidating. My three little Polaroids looked sorrowfully insignificant amid the other polished professional head shots and contact sheets spread across her desk. Seeing the full magnitude I was amazed I even got in the door.

Wilhelmina's office was plastered with imposing black-and-white blowups of all of her top girls. There were Maud Adams, Margaux Hemingway, Janice Dickinson, and a bevy of other big-league beauties. Willie scrutinized my face, then said in her elegant German accent, "Twenty-two is a bit old to start, but you have a good look."

In her no-nonsense manner she plucked a measuring tape from her desk, saying, "34-22-34, good. You'll need to cut your hair, I want you to go to Yoshi, tell him a clean bob to the shoulders.

"We already have two Catherines; how about Katrina," she suggested. I wasn't crazy about Katrina; to me it sounded like a Spanish dancer. She tossed out some more names, and we finally settled on Vanessa. Wilhelmina picked up the phone and set up an appointment for a photo shoot with Patrice, the dashing in-house French photographer. She told me where to buy my little black portfolio and to be sure to call the agency every day by five for my list of "go-sees." Just like that, I walked out of her office a Wilhelmina model.

Becoming a working model wasn't going to be as easy or glamorous as I'd imagined. Living two hours from the city and having a five-year-old to tote along made it all the more challenging.

We had to rise by 5:00 A.M. in order to make the 6:40 train from Brewster, then ride another hour and a half to Grand Central Station. If the train was already pulling out, I'd have to sling Damian on my hip and run for it like our sweet lives depended on us being aboard. I'd do my makeup on the train, being careful not to poke my eye out with the mascara wand while the train bumped and bounced along toward the city. With half an hour before my first appointment I'd take my hair rollers out in the cavernous, Art Deco ladies' room in the station. I'd do the finishing touches of lip gloss and blush under the unflattering fluorescent lights. Trying to look glamorous at eight in the morning was never easy.

Go-sees were my appointments with an array of fashion photographers, and Willie kept me busy pounding the pavement. If a photographer liked your look, he'd do a test shoot; in return I'd get the prints to put together my portfolio.

I think I met with every photographer and ad agency in New York City. I didn't have extra money for a taxi, or even bus fare, so Damian and I hoofed it up and down the avenues. To make matters worse, my little tyke had a fearful aversion to elevators. Whenever I tried to get him into the lift, he'd screech and squeal so loud we'd have to jump out just before the doors closed and scale an arduous twenty or thirty flights of steep stairs. By the end of the day I was weary as Tess of the D'Urbervilles. I'd use my last shred of energy sprinting through the gates at Grand Central Station, just in time to catch the six o'clock back to Connecticut, then do it all over again the next day.

My dedication was paying off. In just three months I had a nice little cache of black-and-white beauty shots and a progress appointment with Willie.

I was stunned when Wilhelmina shuffled through my portfolio and tossed out all but three of my hard-earned photographs. I thought to myself, "I'll just stick them all back in when I get home." Willie must have sensed my dejection, as before I left her office she said something I'll always remember, and which has pertained to all of my endeavors: "Catherine, only show your best work."

She said it's better to show one outstanding photograph than a portfolio full of average shots.

I decided to trust her wisdom and left the average pictures out of my book. Five months later I got my first paid booking, a full-page beauty ad for *Mademoiselle* magazine.

My baby son was now five years old and had started kindergarten at Stadley Ruff Elementary School. Except for my stint as cash register girl at Caldor, we had rarely spent a moment apart. I'd dress him up for school and almost every morning while we waited for the school bus I'd document the start of his day by taking his picture with my Brownie Star Flash camera. Letting him go off on his own was almost unbearable, but there was a benefit. I could now go to my appointments in the city without toting my tot. Wilhelmina was more than gracious and arranged my schedule so that I could be back to Connecticut just in time to meet Damian's school bus as it stopped in front of our cottage.

On one of my appointments I ran into my old friend Miss Pamela, the femme fatale who had charmed Jimmy Page away from my heart in Hollywood. Pamela had since become an actress and was playing the part of Amy, a hippie girl on the soap opera *Search for Tomorrow.* In real life she'd fallen in love again; this time it was with the pretty English rocker and lead singer of Silverhead, Michael Des Barres. She said she was leaving her soap opera and packing it all in to move back to California and become Mrs. Des Barres. It turned out that we were both enthusiastic treasure hunters, and I invited her up to Connecticut for a final weekend of tantalizing barn auctions and tag sales. Pamela discovered a pristine 1940s bamboo dining set for twenty dollars and couldn't resist a deal. She had no idea how she'd get it back to California, but it just wasn't in her to pass up a bargain. Two weeks later Miss Pamela rolled up in a funky blue Cadillac Coupe de Ville to collect her lucky find. She brought along a conservative-looking young man with short blond hair, neatly parted to the side, and horn-rimmed glasses, not at all Miss Pamela's type. She said he was just a friend from her acting class, but he looked besotted to me. He was smitten enough that he had offered to drive her all the way to Hollywood. Her friend, Joseph, rigged the table and unwieldy chairs to the roof of the Caddy, then snapped a few Polaroids of me and Pamela. Pamela took the last shot of Joseph and me in front of the log cabin, and the Beverly Hillbillies were on their way to gold country.

Another one of my enterprises was making delicate little purses from remnants of Victorian velvet, which I painstakingly embroidered with bits of silk and tiny glass beads. I sold them at a ritzy boutique on Main Street in Ridgefield. Life has a plan. Each petite fleur I stitched brought me closer to the man who would send me reeling back home to California. My one-of-a-kind bags were selling like hotcakes, and helped pay my train fare back and forth to the city. I was dropping off a new batch when I was introduced to Chris Walker, a friend of the proprietor of the boutique.

Chris was as beautiful as an angel. He had the palest blue eyes, and soft blond curls encircling his perfect, chiseled face. He was a kid from a well-to-do family in Connecticut. He complimented my purses, and we chatted about the splendor of the lake. What a coincidence: Chris docked his boat on Candlewood, not far from my landing. I casually suggested he might come over for dinner sometime, and he jumped at the invitation.

Wow, a real date! I baked the lamb pie Mrs. Wheeler had taught me, with mashed potatoes instead of biscuits on top, and crisped a gooey, fresh peach cobbler for dessert. I played Mozart full volume, and had a rip-roaring blaze in the fireplace. The table was set with my finest thrift shop linen and Blue Willow dishes. Everything was perfection, except that the guy never showed.

He called the next day saying, "I thought we were going to have dinner."

He said he drove by, but when he saw all the people he decided not to stop. I asked, "What people? Except for Damian I was alone."

"Well, who did all those cars out front belong to?"

Ha! I'd completely forgotten about all my cars! My multicar ruse actually scared somebody off. It worked!

We made new plans to go to the air show over the weekend. Chris dazzled me with little gifts of antique jewelry and fine wines. In less than a month he had essentially moved in with Damian and me.

I was impressed that at twenty-five Chris headed his own business and ran a full crew, planting and restoring botanical landscapes. Being a native of Connecticut, he also knew all the beautiful spots, hidden lakes, and waterfalls to canoe and skinny-dip in. I thought he was the perfect, idyllic gentleman till we drove up to Cape Cod in his XKE Jaguar for the Fourth of July weekend. We were in the midst of a candlelit seafood dinner, when out of the blue he blurted out, "Whadaya think, I'm some kind of idiot?"

I was stunned.

"I see you looking at that guy!"

His angelic face completely morphed into that of a venom-spitting serpent. I barely recognized him.

In mortified disbelief I asked, "What guy, who are you talking about?"

He tossed his money down for the check and pushed away from the table, snarling, "Don't think I'm a fool."

He then proceeded to storm out of the restaurant. I abandoned my king crab legs and chased after him, trying to defend my innocence.

Chris had waited till he was sure I loved him to unleash his frightening little demon, who was just bursting to break loose. His charming ambassador had taken a hike and jealous genes were on the rampage.

Throughout our turbulent relationship it was his practice to rummage through my purse and search my pockets, looking for phantom phone numbers and telltale matchbooks. Before getting home, to save the peace, I'd be sure to purge myself, tossing anything that could be construed as contact with another human being. While I was working away in the city, Chris would rifle through my drawers, pockets, and picture albums. I found my treasured photographs of Jackson Browne torn to shreds. Any other unidentified male photos, including those of my own brother, shared the same fate. He'd call the studio at my modeling bookings, insinuating I was having sex with the photographer, and would sometimes even show up in the city, parked outside, hoping to catch me in the imagined act. Why in the world was I holding on to another man who acted crazy and was clearly tortured? But when he was rational he could charm the devil. I was also hopelessly attracted to his handsome face and hoped he'd eventually mellow out. It seemed almost impossible that I'd moved all the way from England to an obscure plot in Connecticut and managed to find an exact emotional replica of Denny Laine. I started to wonder, was it something about me? I felt panicky and anxious, the same feeling I had had living with my mother. Whenever I suggested that Chris get his own place, he'd turn back to charmer mode, and I'd let it go. Maybe I was comfortable with the Jekyll-and-Hyde drama. Was I looking for grief or was grief looking for me? Whatever it was, I needed to make a change.

While trying to extricate myself from my sticky entanglement I found solace in watching TV soap operas. During the mornings when I didn't have to be in the city, and Chris was at work restoring the gardens of rural Connecticut, I'd tune into *As the World Turns*, and soon developed a crackpot crush on Dr. Dan Stewart of Oakdale General Memorial. Dr. Dan was kind, caring, and compassionate, everything Chris wasn't. My pipe-dream fantasy man actually made my stormy relationship with Chris almost bearable. I was well aware that Dr. Dan was purely an actor on television, but I decided to send John Reilly a letter at CBS, along with my beguiling modeling card from Wilhelmina, suggesting we meet for lunch. I imagined us meeting at the romantic Tavern on the Green, ensconced in dreamy, meaningful conversation. Dr. Dan would save the day. I actually wrote the letter, and for fear of Chris discovering my adulterous heart, I kept the letter hidden deep in the lining of my winter coat.

Christmas morning of 1974 started off like a fairy tale. The snow was falling, and wind was blowing crystals off the ice on the frozen lake. Little Damian was up before dawn, making mouse tears in every present under the tree. He couldn't wait to see if Santa had brought the Steve Austin *Six Million Dollar Man* action figure and the matching bionic repair station he was hoping for. Chris surprised me with the cherry red platform sandals I'd been eyeing at Ann Taylor, and I bought him an assortment of art books and a vintage smoking jacket. This seemed to be the happy Christmas I'd always imagined. The fireplace was crackling with the smell of pine, Damian was happily ensconced with Santa's offerings, and I was in the kitchen stuffing a plump turkey for the oven. Then, for no apparent reason, or maybe because he was disappointed with his presents, Chris went into one of his inexplicable rages and tossed all his Christmas gifts into the fire. While I tried to retrieve a book from the flames, Chris snatched the red shoes he had bought me and pitched them in the lake one at a time before speeding off in his XKE Jaguar. Little did he know that that was his last scene and final exit. I'd hoped he was gone for good, but he showed up the next morning like nothing had happened. When I handed him his packed bags, he went into another tirade and scowled, "I'm not going anywhere; this is my place."

He said that if I didn't like it, I could move. I could see this wasn't going to end gracefully and wasn't sure he'd even let me go. I was fresh out of energy for conflict, and decided it might be easier to let him come back until I came up with a solution. In desperation I called my eccentric aunt Claire in Los Angeles.

"You know you always have a home here; I don't know what you're doing up in the sticks anyway!"

I secretly began planning and plotting my getaway. Chris could have the place. I was going home to California. Unfortunately, I'd recently bred my Russian wolfhound, Molly, who'd just given birth to fifteen puppies, about ten more than I'd expected. Borzois aren't small dogs, and I couldn't take them all with me to California. I cleared out my sewing room and used the fireplace screen to keep the pups from running riot and obliterating the house. At just five weeks old, they had already figured out how to get over the makeshift barrier. When Damian and I would get home from my go-sees in the city, the click of my key in the door would cause a stampede that sounded like a cattle drive. Three times a day I'd fill the deep turkey pan to the hilt with sweet milk, and the pups devoured the liquid in less then a minute; then all fifteen would poop and pee in distressing unison.

My God, how were we going to get out of here with all these puppies? It seemed like they grew an inch a day, and no matter how high I raised the barricade, all fifteen little black noses romped at the front door, waiting to greet me.

I put an ad in *The New York Times* and got a flurry of responses. People came from as far as Vermont to buy my homegrown brood.

I sold the MGA and the Mini Cooper, but left the old Humber and Volkswagen so as not to raise suspicion. When a young girl showed up for the Pontiac with a baby in her arms, I got a certain delight in telling her that it was hers for free.

I called a drive-away company that just happened to have a station wagon that needed to be driven to California. I rented a small U-Haul trailer, hitched it to the wagon, and parked it out of sight. When Chris drove off to work in the morning I packed the U-Haul to the rafters. By dusk, in the midst of another snowstorm, Damian and I were slipping and sliding our way back to the West, with the last four Russian wolfhounds plus Molly frolicking in the back seat.

After four days and five thousand miles, my son and I arrived safe and sound at my aunt Claire's home on Ozeta Terrace.

I hadn't been back here since the last time I saw my dad, the night he took me on Mr. Toad's Wild Ride fifteen years earlier. The lovely old iron gates were rusting, and the once lush, green lawn was unkempt and overgrown. The weathered old Cadillacs were still in the garage, but by now they had turned into collectors' items. The place had the eerie feeling of *What Ever Happened to Baby Jane?*

Aunt Claire wasn't home yet, but my fading old gran Helen greeted me at the door with open arms.

I introduced her to her first great-grandson, and she seemed overjoyed. I put my four wolfhounds out on the terrace and unpacked some of my things while she made us tea and sandwiches. It felt good to be back there. I'd almost forgotten I had a family, even a little history, here.

We were having a nice chat in the dining room and enjoying the peanut-butter-and-jelly fare when I asked my grandmother Helen, "Does my dad know I'm here yet?"

She got the oddest look on her pale, sweet face.

"What was your last name, dear?" she asked.

This little woman had invited us into her home, allowed me to move my belongings in, and had just made us lunch. Sadly, I realized she didn't have a clue who we were. I softly said, "James, grandmother, just like yours."

Her blue eyes sparkled like a bell had gone off, but her once-sharp mind had been ravaged by dementia.

There was something wonderful and almost macabre about coming back to Ozeta Terrace. It was strange revisiting a past that hadn't moved forward. Everything was exactly the same as the last time I had been here. Besides a later model television set in the living room, there was little evidence we were in the midseventies. The heavy curtains were drawn shut and the chimes of the mantel clock tolled as if they were mourning a death.

Claire soon arrived, laden with shopping bags, and her son, Blake, still close to her heels. Blake and I were the same age. At twenty-seven he had the makings of a handsome young man, but there was something odd about him. He was a gawky six-foot-two with awkward body language, as if he was afraid to make a wrong move. His complexion was ghostly pallid, sort of moist, like he never saw the sun. Blake wasn't really overweight, but his physique had a rounded, sexless cast, and his clothes were shapeless and unkempt. I don't think he even had had a friend since graduating Black Foxe military school. Blake was all that Claire had left, and she selfishly kept him bound and tied close to her apron strings, via her purse. Even though the house had five spacious bedrooms and a separate apartment downstairs, for some wacky reason they shared the twin beds in my grandparents' old quarters. I could see that Blake was a breath away from becoming a shut-in; he had never held a job or had a dream of his own. He twisted and turned trying to free himself from his mother's cloying clutches, but when he tried to make a move on his own, Claire threatened to disinherit him and leave her declining estate to the Motion Picture & Television Home. When we were alone he confided that he'd never even been kissed. He was still pure and chaste, a virgin with little hope for a girl or a life of his own.

Aunt Claire was showing some age but still possessed her beautiful, flawless face. Even for a midnight trip to Ralph's supermarket she got made up dramatically and dressed to the nines, always ready for her close-up. She still painted on luscious Lucy lips and powdered her poreless skin to perfection. Her long lashes were spiked with thick layers of Aziza, the old studio mascara that used to come in a blue box. She'd spit in the palette till it got gooey, then apply several coats with the stiff little brush.

Claire couldn't bear to throw anything away, and her faded pink dressing room looked like the Max Factor Museum. Her shelves and dresser tops were three deep in original Deco bottles and lotion jars. There were vanishing creams, powders, and half-empty sachets of White Shoulders and Chanel No. 5 perfume. I'd never seen such an amazing collection. All the half-filled and used-up milky, colored bottles were like a life's journal. The round mirror above the vanity had reflected fifty-three years: the young hopeful starlet, three stormy marriages, and now an eccentric, aging beauty queen.

Claire toiled away in the kitchen, using the old institution-sized cooking pots, and at midnight dinner was served. She plopped a heaping platter piled high with spaghetti and giant-sized meatballs in front of me, then brought out four more overflowing trays. There was literally enough spaghetti for thirty people. I said, "Wow, this is a lot of food, Claire!"

She yelled back, "Well, you better eat it!"

Nobody ever spoke softly in this house. Even when I was a child everyone shouted as if they were hard of hearing; it was actually pretty comical. After dinner Claire and Blake took turns disappearing outside to the surrounding terrace, leaving me to sit with my grandmother Helen, whose blue eyes were permanently transfixed in the twilight zone. I peeped out to see what was so fascinating on the verandah and saw Claire sneaking a nip, then stashing her tumbler under the ledge. They were both secret alcoholics, hiding it from each other in their own house. I wondered, "Would I have turned out like them if I had stayed on here, if I never ran away?"

Damian and I were quite comfortable in the guest quarters downstairs, but when we'd leave the house, Aunt Claire would come down and rearrange my belongings, shut the windows, and draw all the drapes shut. I was mystified to find that while we were out she had cut the electrical cords clean off my alarm clock and electric hair rollers. It was her kooky way of letting me know that I was using too much electricity.

The biggest bombshell came when Aunt Claire and Blake were getting ready to go to the airport. I asked who they were picking up. Claire huffed, like it was a big bother, "Oh, it's Bob's other daughter."

I had to think for a minute: Bob's other daughter, what other daughter?

Claire said my dad had had an affair twenty years ago, and now the girl wanted to meet her father. In utter astonishment, I asked, "Wouldn't that make her my sister, then?"

Claire thought about this, then said, "I guess she would be."

Wow. I had a sister who lived in Colorado, and nobody had ever thought to tell me.

We met Carol at LAX airport, and she was the spitting image of my dad, a tall blond Swede with pale blue eyes. Her demeanor was simple and shy. She was soft-spoken, with clear, innocent eyes, not at all like anyone in my family. Carol had clearly been sheltered, and traditionally cared for. She knew nothing about Hollywood or the eccentric James family. She just wanted to meet her long-lost father. Unbelievably, Aunt Claire hadn't mentioned to my dad that she was bringing Carol to his home; Claire just plopped her off on his front door. The hapless reunion must have been a shocker to my dad. He refused even to open the front door. I felt mortified for Carol, and tried to console her. I tried to persuade her not to take it personally, but I knew it was a moment she would carry to the grave. We exchanged telephone numbers, she boarded the jet plane, and I never saw my sister again.

13

I felt like Marilyn, the normal niece of the Munster family. I quickly realized that Damian and I needed to find a place of our own, pronto!

I started my rounds with Wilhelmina's Los Angeles agency, and found that my eighty million go-sees in New York had paid off. On my first interview I booked three weeks' work on a Saks Fifth Avenue catalog.

I rented a roomy Spanish-style house on Kirkwood Avenue in Laurel Canyon, and was happy to finally unpack my things and have a bit of solitude. I enrolled my eight-year-old son in Wonderland Avenue Elementary School, and began working full-time doing layouts for Bloomingdale's, Macy's, and I. Magnin. For the first time I was making more money than I had time to spend. I bought a classic 1964 red MGA convertible for two thousand cash, and stashed the rest under my mattress and between book pages, like my grandmother Mimi did.

* * *

It was 1976 and New Year's Eve. I was invited to a fancy bash at an artist's loft in downtown Los Angeles. I had a touch of the flu and wasn't really up for a party, but something urged me to go. I slipped on some pencil-thin velvet trousers, an off-the-shoulder Marilyn sweater, and a scant pair of spiked slides. I grabbed a few strands of silver tinsel from our Christmas tree and fixed it in a festive bow encircling my neck, and I was ready to meet the new year.

The trendy warehouse was jam-packed, shoulder-to-shoulder with leggy models, fashion photographers, and interesting artisans. It was a drug-induced fashionable Babylon with the Ronettes' "Frosty the Snowman" blasting through the entire neighborhood. Just before midnight I edged my way past the cocaine line to the powder room and slipped out onto the fire escape for a breath of fresh air. I thought I was alone, but then heard a young man's voice sigh. "Thank you for coming out tonight."

I'd never heard that line before, and couldn't help but smile. He asked, "Would you wait here for one minute?"

Then he came back with my favorite champagne, a hand-painted Art Nouveau bottle of Perrier Jouet, and two glasses for a new year's toast. We were the last to leave the party, and at the end of the night I gave him my telephone number.

Paul Zacha was different from any man I'd ever known. His father was the head art director on the popular show *Dallas*, and Paul was following in his footsteps. Besides being a talented artist and budding art director, he was ridiculously funny. From the moment he'd pick me up he'd have me laughing with artful pratfalls and goofy practical jokes. At a fancy restaurant he took realistic-looking fake flies and floated them in his soup, and strategically planted a few in my pasta. When the waiter came by gasping with apologies, we were in hysterics. He could juggle, perform magic tricks, and lasso anything that moved. Paul also treated my son like he was his own, surprising him with prime Dodgers tickets, playing catch at the park, and hiring him to assist on the film sets he was art directing on. When he was working on a film he'd send a production assistant with chocolate chip ice cream from Baskin-Robbins to my house because that's what I liked for breakfast. He did everything he could think of to impress me, and quickly won my heart. Paul was twenty-seven years old and whimsically romantic. He called me Mrs. Pixley and would muse, "Mrs. Pixley, one day I'm going to buy you a big sparkling diamond ring just like the one my dad gave to my mother," and I would giggle with delight.

My rented house in Laurel Canyon was about to be sold, and I found a charming Deco apartment in the foothills of old Hollywood. Damian and I moved in temporarily with Michael and Pamela Des Barres, and Paul would stay with a friend till our new place was renovated, then we planned to set up house and marry.

It was the late seventies, and cocaine reigned supreme in the inner sanctums and on film sets. I did my share, but Paul became insatiable. We'd been together for almost two years, but it wasn't just us anymore; wherever we went, whatever we did, the insidious vial of powder came along with us. We'd have fascinating, cocaine-induced, meaningless conversations till dawn. I'd try to fall asleep before sunrise with my heart pulsating clear to the bedsprings. I'd make deals with God praying, "Please don't let me have a heart attack tonight. I promise I won't do this again."

I'd appeal to Paul, "Let's not do this anymore."

He'd humor me, then stay out till the wee hours under the guise of working late.

Paul had just been hired to art direct a period movie, and the production company advanced him five thousand in petty cash. When I learned he'd spent a thousand of it on cocaine, I flipped.

"This is it," he promised. "When this is finished I'm done, just one last weekend."

I tossed every ruinous affront I could sling, then slammed the phone down in his ear. I eventually regained my composure and remembered that I loved him, and should have been more supportive. I decided to let him have his night, and would call him the next day to make amends.

I spent the morning with my son happily combing the Saturday flea market and estate sales for unfound treasures, but when I got home Pamela seemed abnormally upset.

"I have something really bad to tell you," she said.

I asked, "What?" But she couldn't bring herself to say the words. The somber look on her face was as serious as heart failure.

"Pamela, you're starting to scare me, what's wrong?"

There was a long pause, then the sickening words, "Paul is dead."

I instantly felt like vomiting, but calmly replied, "Don't say that! He's not dead."

"I'm so sorry," she said. "His sister called while you were out; he died last night of a heart attack. It was a cocaine overdose."

He couldn't be dead, we were young and invincible, we were both only twenty-nine years old. Then I remembered three days ago, when he asked me to read his palm.

He questioned, "Do you think I'll have a long life?"

I touched the lines in the inside of his slender hand and saw nothing.

"I don't know," I said. "I don't get a feeling."

He clasped my hand and sweetly said, "I hope I die before you; I wouldn't want to be on the Earth without you."

I'd never been one to give up or take no for an answer, but death was an impermeable barrier I couldn't cross. If I didn't have an eleven-year-old son to raise, I might have followed, taken the leap and tried to catch up with him. My snappy last words ate at my soul like ravenous demons. I prayed and implored God that he knew I didn't mean a word of it, that he left the world knowing I loved him.

I took to haunting the liquor aisles, swigging tart bottles of wine, trying to drown the bitter contrition, but nothing could console me.

After Paul's memorial his family asked me if there was anything I wanted from his belongings. Besides one of his unfinished paintings, Paul left a Deco ceramic pot planted with three miniature palm trees that he'd carefully tended for the previous ten years. I've managed to keep the palms flourishing in the same pottery for twenty-four years, and now they are a willowy five feet tall. Most important, Paul left me with an invaluable gift. When I slammed the phone down on him I never dreamed in a million years it would be my last gesture. That was the hardest and most painful part of his death, the way I left it. From that day since I've never left anyone with an unkind word or without being crystal clear about my feelings. I think of Paul every time some-one walks out my door.

14

*P*amela's husband, Michael, was on tour with his band, Checkered Past, which gave Pamela plenty of time to do what she liked best: go shopping. After scouring the thrift shops in the depths of the San Fernando Valley, she came home saying, "Do you remember that guy I brought up to your house in Connecticut?"

I laughed. "Yeah, the goofy guy with the glasses, the one who drove you all the way to California."

She told me she had run into him out on Lankershim Boulevard, and he was coming over to treat us to a spicy Thai dinner.

Joseph rolled up in his Volkswagen square-back wearing the same funky horn rims, and dressed in nondescript casual attire. I thought he still fancied Pamela, but all through dinner he unabashedly stared directly into my eyes. Even when I burst out with laughter, he held his curious, fixed gaze. I whispered to Pamela, "What a weirdo."

She laughed, "Come on, be nice. He's coming over Friday to help us with our yard sale."

Pamela's and my wealth of vintage crapola was enough to stock a medium-sized flea market, and our yard sales were a neighborhood event. Literally, by 7:00 A.M., a hundred bargain hunters would be gathered, chomping at the bit for us to open the gates. Friday evening, while sorting through the spoils, Joseph took a fancy to one of Michael's 1950s suits. It was a gold lamé Elvis ensemble that fit him like it was tailor-made. With no shirt and the shimmering jacket hanging loosely open, his smooth chest was like that of a dreamy Adonis. Without the horn-rims, he stood in the doorway wielding Michael's guitar and purring a sexy rendition of "Blue Suede Shoes": "One for the money, two for the show." In a magical moment he'd gone from Clark Kent to a sensual god who had my full attention.

In the midst of the morning yard sale frenzy an amazing thing happened: One of the hagglers came up to me and asked, "Is your name Catherine?"

When I confessed, the man said he used to be a resident at Vista del Mar, the orphanage I had lived at. After all these years I couldn't believe that this guy had recognized me. He said he remembered the time I brought Bob Dylan onto the grounds and what a stir I'd caused. Ha! I remembered how all the ungracious delinquents scoffed and jeered at Bob that day in 1963, and how humiliated I had felt. I couldn't help but reiterate my prophetic words, "I told you you'd never forget it."

He also said that I'd been a bit of a legend. I was the wild girl, and the only one who ever ran away from that place and got away with it. I'd come full circle. He paid his fifty cents for a worn copy of the Beatles' *Rubber Soul* and disappeared back into the past.

After an exhausting, sweaty ten-hour day of selling, haggling, and finally packing up the last unwanted dregs of the sale, I offered to make Joseph dinner for all his gracious help. Any other time I would have paid cold cash just to be able to go straight to sleep, but the feeling of looming romance promptly revived my spirit. In the flip of a coin, I'd gone from thinking he was a goofball to feeling like a nervous schoolgirl trying to make my best impression. I prepared us a delicious pot of Indian curry, and before I knew it we were in my bed having the most passionate sex I'd ever experienced. It lasted till the sun rose. We would have gone on, but Joseph had to go. He had a morning flight from LAX to visit his parents in Oregon.

Joseph was an actor who had done a handful of commercials and acted in local theater. He supplemented his living as a skilled-finish carpenter. He owned a Craftsman house in Santa Monica that was a perpetual work in progress. The decor was bachelor Zen. No sofas or carpets, just clean space with a simple bed and a chest of drawers he'd built from scratch. There was an old upright piano in the living room with a small, framed photograph on top. When I looked closer I was amazed; it was the picture Pamela had taken of us six years earlier in front of my house in Connecticut. Were we predestined?

Joseph came from a place I'd only dreamed of. He'd never tasted alcohol or puffed on a cigarette, or had any other sort of contraband. He'd grown up in a large cozy family in rural Oregon, and still attended church services on Sundays. He was John Boy in the flesh, or maybe he was Jesus in disguise.

I don't know how I missed it in the beginning, but Joseph was the most handsome man I'd ever laid eyes on, with clear blue eyes and baby blond hair. His graceful hands looked like the work of Michelangelo. We had a chemistry I'd never expected or experienced. We made love like gods till dawn, then we'd wake up and do it again. Sex with Joseph was like time traveling, rocketing out of my body and finding myself hovering in a meadow, or an awareness of being in another century. I never knew where we'd go, but I couldn't get there without him. He was like a liberating euphoric drug, and I was thoroughly hooked.

I finally moved into my new apartment on El Cerrito Place, and Joseph rented out his Santa Monica digs to move in with me. We joined the old Methodist church on the corner of Franklin and Highland that had the most elaborate, grand pipe organ in all of California. Joseph joined the men's morning prayer group and we attended all the holiday parties and Sunday teas. The dances were held in the church gymnasium and were wonderfully hokey, like going back to the innocent times of the fifties. On Valentine's Day the hall was decked in red construction paper hearts and pink spiraling streamers. Heart-shaped sugar biscuits and sweet strawberry punch were the refreshments. Joseph and I did the swing to Bobby Darin's "Queen of the Hop," and we slow danced to Patsy Cline's "Sweet Dreams (of You)." It was the mideighties but you'd never know it.

Unfortunately, my son was not as enamored as I was. He was approaching the terrible teens and had become most comfortable ruling the roost, having me all to himself. He admired Joseph, but when Joseph started laying down the laws, my young son bucked like a wild bronco. When Joseph stood firm on reasonable rules, my son changed his strategy, and I became the enemy. In secrecy he'd confide to my new boyfriend, "Wait until you get to really know her, you'll be sorry."

During an afternoon brunch at the farmers' market on Fairfax, young master Damian took the opportunity to remark, "You're starting to look really old, mom. How come your hands look so wrinkly?" I was mortified.

From the moment my son was born I had lived for him, and wanted to give him everything I never had. It was through him that I loved myself. Damian was my purpose and grounding force, but when I fell in love with Joseph, my little dream boy turned into a nightmare. He was pushing hard for me to choose between him and Joseph, but there had to be an easier alternative.

It was coming on Christmas, and Joseph invited us to go to Oregon for the holidays to meet his family. I wanted to go more than anything, but what was I going to do about my salty son? He was as grumpy as a riled tiger and definitely not the picture I wanted to present to Joseph's family.

I rarely saw my younger brother, Scot, but we always kept in contact by telephone. He'd recently married his eighteen-year-old girlfriend, Gina, and had moved to an idyllic little house in the mountains near Lake Tahoe. It was the perfect solution. I'd send my surly cub to spend Christmas with my brother. He could cool his heels in the mountainous country snow.

Joseph and I drove the sixteen hours to his family's home in Gresham, Oregon. Instead of stopping halfway at a common inn, we camped out in the wintry forest. I'm sure we were the only souls camping in the frosted timberlands in mid-December, but it was far more romantic than any wayside lodge. In the morning we came upon a picturesque bridge spanning a deep river. We stripped off our clothes, grabbed each other's hand, and jumped off the trestle. I've never gotten out of the water faster. The current was so cold that the December air actually felt warm on our wet bodies.

We arrived safely at the farm in Oregon, and I finally got to meet Joseph's affectionate family. There were four brothers and an older sister. His father was a part-time missionary and his mother played the organ at the local church. After the Christmas candlelight church service, the whole family went door-to-door, singing Christmas carols in the descending snow. The feeling of being part of this, the sense of belonging, was so unlike anything I'd grown up with, it was almost indescribable.

Joseph woke me up at dawn whispering, "Catherine, come to the window, look at the sunrise."

That's what I loved so much about Joseph; he always saw and took time to inhale the beauty. We made slow, quiet love, being careful not to disturb the squeaky floorboards till his mom called us down for pancakes.

Christmas morning all the kids, grandkids, nieces, and nephews were there to open their presents. I had bought Joseph a fancy alarm clock from ritzy Fred Segal's, and he got me the flowing white, night-gown I'd seen in the Bloomingdale's catalog, the one with the baby blue, double-back satin ribbon. Later we all packed into the family pickup loaded down with massive black inner tubes to sled the slopes by the farm. This was truly the most perfect time in my life.

We went back to Oregon for the Fourth of July holiday and Damian happily went back to visit with my brother and his wife, Gina. Oregon in the summer was just as idyllic as at Christmas. This time it was warm enough to skinny-dip in the waters of Lake Shasta. At his family's farm we played softball in the endless green fields, and drifted down a balmy river in the same rubber tubes we had sledded with in December. To help a neighboring farm we picked bushels and baskets of sweet ripe raspberries before they spoiled. With the extra berries, Joseph's mother taught me how to bake a stunning fruit cobbler, and make my very own homemade jam, which I was quite proud of. After the holiday we boarded a train, the Coast Starlight, back to California, and splurged on a private sleeping compartment. It was in this glori-ous wee room where Joseph with his Gary Cooper charm spoke the words, "I was thinkin' we should get married."

Marry him? I would have followed this man through eternal hell-fire. He said, "Yep, sometimes those Hollywood marriages just don't work out. We might have to move back to Oregon."

I was afraid to shut my eyes in case it was a dream. We didn't sleep a wink but made glorious love the whole twenty-two-hour ride home.

Three months later we were married by a lake on the coast of Oregon. Moments before our wedding a ladybug landed on Joseph's sleeve. What was so amazing about this little bug, and I swear this is true, is that instead of the usual little black dots on the wings, this one had two perfectly shaped hearts, one on each wing. As we walked toward the lake for the communion, Joseph handed me a small folded note that read "I've seen the beauty on the earth and in the skies but it doesn't match the beauty of what I see in your eyes."

I was almost unconscious with sweet euphoria.

We honeymooned at a country inn on an ancient Indian reservation. The land was surrounded by natural hot springs and dotted with authentic tepees. It was the first and only time I ever got Joseph to stay in a hotel with grand room service and all. If he'd had his druthers, we would have camped under the moonlight and stars.

We drove home via the coast, winding through Big Sur and Monterey, stopping to visit all the quaint roadside antique shops and rustic inns. The whole heavenly drive I couldn't stop staring at my wedding ring finger. I think I formed a new-sprung muscle from holding my hand out so long, admiring the luminous golden band with glorious delight. We were really married. I had finally found my prince; would it be like this forever?

We didn't get back to Hollywood till two in the morning, and were too tired to even unpack. We dragged our bags and wedding booty into the sitting room and went directly to blissful slumber.

At 5:00 A.M., we were awoken by a startling ring. It was Joseph's dad on the telephone. Their conversation lasted less than a minute, then Joseph put his face to the pillow and sobbed deep, inconsolable tears. His beloved older brother, James, had been hit by a drunk driver on his motorcycle, and had died in a field by the side of the road in Oregon.

We'd been married just five little days ago, and now we were on our way back to Oregon for a funeral. It was almost unbearable to see Joseph in such despair. Even worse, he refused to be comforted and only wanted to be left alone. It was exactly like someone had died. With a blink of an eye, the joy was gone.

After a while the clouds began to clear, but it was never the same. We hardly spoke and rarely made love anymore. I'd fix his breakfast in the morning and bake his favorite desserts. I'd iron his shirts and stick little Post-it notes on the collar saying how handsome he looked in them, but I couldn't get his attention. I was trying to remind him of the girl he had fallen in love with, but he only got more distant. I held in my sadness, still trying to be the perfect, loving wife, but it all seemed to be in vain.

About the same time, something strange began to happen. It started off when I was making a batch of tomato sauce. The can of crushed tomatoes tasted slightly off, so I checked the date, and found it had long expired. I remembered reading something about botulism and canned tomatoes, and went into a panic. I quickly called the poison control hotline and inquired, "How much tainted tomato sauce would one have to eat to get botulism?"

In a calm, pleasant voice the woman on the phone said, "Oh, just a taste could kill you, dear."

Oh my God, I'd already ingested two large spoonfuls, and was sure I was doomed. With my stomach beginning to ache, I dumped the whole pot down the drain and jumped into bed, waiting to succumb. After that trauma, any kind of fish became the culprit, then canned goods, then dairy products, and finally any meat became the enemy. I even stopped taking vitamins for fear they'd been tampered with. I eventually found the vomitorium more pleasurable than fine dining, and kept this little secret all to myself. I didn't know what was happening to me, but I'd convinced myself, even with all my precautions, that I would end up being accidentally poisoned.

When Joseph was finally ready to talk, it was to say he needed some time to himself, maybe he should move out for a few months, until he felt better. I had a suspicion there was more to this story; when someone moves out, it's rare that they move back in. I asked Joseph the age-old question, "Is it another woman?"

He looked at me like I was depraved for even having such absurd thoughts. "How could you be so ridiculous and insecure?" he huffed.

This was the man I had just married, the man I loved and trusted. I was bewildered but, wanting to believe him, assured him he was free to go, whatever it took for us to be happy again.

Shortly after that conversation, I was headed to Santa Monica in my Triumph convertible when a street peddler approached my car with bags of tempting fat cherries for sale. I'd finished half the bag before the voice of insanity loomed, "How could you have bought fruit from a stranger?"

The cherries were surely contaminated. I pulled my car to the curb and started carefully inspecting each one for puncture marks. Sadly, it looked as if every single one was adulterated with some kind of suspect spot, but it was too late to heave. Surely the poisonous toxins would have already begun to take effect. In the midst of my hysteria, I had a moment of clarity. There I was parked on a side street in terrified tears, picking through cherries like some kind of lunatic. I realized it wasn't the cherries, it was me. I needed help.

I lucked out and found Dr. Thomas Deshler, an insightful therapist at Cedars-Sinai Medical Center. I thought it would be a casual visit, like a checkup, but I was in for a surprise.

I could usually charm the pants off any stranger, but this doctor wasn't there to be enchanted. He gently suggested, "Why don't we start from the very beginning."

The beginning didn't seem that important; my problem was now. I was afraid to eat anything, and if I did, I got so paranoid I'd have to throw it up before the assumed toxins reached my bloodstream. I knew that it sounded ridiculous, but the fear was real and overwhelming. I was starving to death. I casually spoke of my childhood, revealing a few tidbits about my mother. I glossed over how she used to keep me locked in the closet or bound tight in a chair. How she disciplined her little girl by forcing her to eat Ivory soap bars and swigs of Tabasco. By the time I got to her abandoning me at the train yard in the night, I had big salty teardrops running down my cheeks. Hearing my own words was heartbreaking, like I was talking about someone else, then realized it was me. I'd never really spoken about the frightful early years, and apologized for my unexpected outburst. He handed me a box of tissues and I wept like that long lost baby girl. After blowing my stuffed-up nose several times, and thankfully regaining my composure, I said, "Actually, I'm just here for the food poisoning problem."

Joseph rented a garage apartment in Studio City and we began dating. We still made love, but instead of being joyous, it was heartrending, like each time was going to be the last. He swore there was no one else, but I could feel it in my soul; he no longer belonged to me.

Finally, someone came to my emotional rescue and offered me the lowdown on my bewildered marriage. Oddly enough it was a friend of Joseph's, a girl that I'd met in Oregon when we first started going out. I was spilling out my dazed heart to her when she stopped me, and asked, "Do you really want to know what's going on?"

My heart started to race. Yes, more than anything I wanted to know. She told me my husband was having an affair with a girl he'd met at a commercial audition. She was an actress. In a strange way it took me out of my confused misery. At least I knew what I was up against. I looked her up in the Screen Actors Guild directory and called her agent, posing as a television producer. Her agent sent me a package of head shots and a résumé, which I studied like a private eye. Who was this immoral witch? It certainly couldn't have been her physical beauty that had captivated my husband. She was a freckle-faced redhead. I'd lie awake at night and imagine myself going to her house with a gun. Of course, I didn't own a gun, nor would I ever shoot anyone, but the visual of her opening the front door and me standing there, pointing a threatening pistol at her heart, gave mine a twisted momentary feeling of empowerment. Homicide was a bit excessive, but I wasn't going down easy. I sent her a poignant letter appealing to her decency, or lack of it. I honestly thought if she knew I had a name, a human heartbeat, she might see the evil of her immoral ways and relent, give my husband back.

The other woman had been a soap actress. She had appeared on *Days of Our Lives*, but now had a recurring role on a popular television show. Masochistically, I never missed a Tuesday night episode. I even paid to see a dreary play she was appearing in just to get a closer look at her face in person. I took solace in despising her, ripping apart her mediocre acting, but the grim truth was that she had bewitched my husband, and there was not a thing I could do about it. In my missive I wrote a modest reference to karmic justice, action and reaction. I was absolutely cheerful when two weeks after I sent her my letter, her show was mysteriously canceled and she was out of a job.

It was coming on Christmas, the time when Joseph and I usually headed for Oregon. We were still dating, even making love, but when he announced he was taking the actress instead of me, it was more than I could bear. We had just gotten married there—three months ago. It was actually less agonizing when my boyfriend Paul died of the drug overdose; at least there was finality, a clear-cut closure. Joseph, my husband, was alive and making love with another woman just a few miles down the road. I refused to believe he just ceased being in love with me. The cosmos was calling, it was time to move on, but it was so painful to let go.

I found myself pursuing the liquor stores again. The truth was, I hated the taste of alcohol. I'd buy cheap sweet port or a bottle of sickly-sweet Frangelico and swig down the whole bottle, anything to deaden the rip-roaring sorrow. I daydreamed of going to a hypnotist and having Joseph's memory eradicated from my aching heart.

In the following three months I lost fifteen pounds in grief, and my modeling jobs were few and far between. Wilhelmina still sent me on interviews, but there was a whole new crop of young beauties, all ten years younger than I was and vying for the same handful of print jobs. My desire to compete for my husband and a livelihood was waning. I needed a change of venue, a stress-free situation.

I'd always been fond of fresh flowers and had a talent for artful arrangements. I applied for a position at the chic LaCienega flower shop on Melrose Avenue. They had the most extensive array of exotic blossoms, and I thought the environment might cheer me up a bit. I remembered how I used to feel receiving a romantic bouquet, and took great pleasure in fashioning grand arrangements for would-be beaus and hopeful suitors. It seemed just about every handsome man in Hollywood frequented the flower shop, but unfortunately most of them were already taken.

During my flower stint, an amazing thing happened. Remember my fantasy TV romance in Connecticut? Dr. Dan Stewart, the soap star doctor from *As the World Turns*? When Dr. Dan breezed into the shop for a dozen roses, I felt like a deer in the headlights. Seeing him in person, away from Oakdale Memorial, smack dab on the middle of Melrose Avenue, was completely out of context. He hadn't a clue of the comforting role he'd played in my mixed-up life in Connecticut, or our imaginary romantic history. John Reilly was true to his soap opera character, warm and friendly, even a little flirtatious, which made my day. I tied an extra-special bow around his wreath of roses, and he left the shop completely unaware of our prior relationship. I never did get the courage to mail my letter to him. It's probably still hidden somewhere in the lining of my winter coat, which I donated years ago.

My new employment and extended psychoanalysis took the edge off my dining drama. I continued my sessions with Dr. Deshler, but instead of our usual office visits, as part of my food-anxiety therapy we began meeting at a little café across from Cedars-Sinai hospital. At one of our afternoon luncheons I was devouring my burger and fries like a ravenous piglet when Dr. Deshler asked, "How do you know the food isn't poisoned here?"

I had to think for a minute. It hadn't even occurred to me to check for contaminants. I suppose I felt safe with him. Nothing bad was going to happen while I was with Dr. Tom. My terror of being poisoned seemed to be a bizarre manifestation of panic. My fear of loss, losing my husband, and myself. My inner voice was clamoring, "You're consuming too much crap!" Like the kindly woman at poison control had warned, "Just a taste could kill you, dear."

After two years of visits with Dr. Deshler, and with Joseph gone from my life, I could finally sit through a meal without knowing the precise route to the vomitorium.

15

After a lifetime of concealed boozing, my eccentric aunt Claire finally succumbed to the swill. She died at sixty-five of cirrhosis of the liver. No one had thought to mention it to me at the time, but my grandmother Helen was also gone. Alzheimer's disease finally got her. My poor defeated cousin was now left to haunt the halls of our decaying house all alone.

For Claire's funeral, Blake dressed his domineering mother in one of her vintage white fox furs, and had her made up like an aging femme fatale. Instead of being laid out, he had her propped up in the casket and surrounded by her beauty pageant trophies and dramatic glamour portraits. It was a scene worthy of Hitchcock's *Psycho*.

Blake was left with a huge house and plenty of cash, but not a clue about how to take care of himself or what to do with his inexperienced life. At thirty-three he'd still never been with a woman, and he started hanging out on Sunset Strip to make friends. He quickly became popular with the local drug hounds, who introduced him to the wonders of cocaine and crystal meth. The home above Sunset that had once been an oasis was now a ransacked flophouse, with drug addicts coming and going at all hours of the day and night. Blake took down his mother's oil portraits and used the canvases to stub out his cigarette butts into the shape of massive pyramids. Besides being confused, I think someplace inside himself he knew she had cheated him of a life.

His final hurrah lasted just six months. He was partying in Santa Monica with a young woman, who was driving his Mercedes. She was too intoxicated to notice the stoplight, and slammed hard into a halted panel truck at sixty miles an hour. Ironically, it was Blake who saved the female driver's life. With no seatbelt, he was hurled in front of the steering wheel. He had cushioned his companion, and took a fatal blow to his chest. The girl walked away unscathed, but my cousin died on impact; sadly, he had never really lived.

My dad had always wanted control of the house on Ozeta Terrace. Years earlier, Claire had been offered over a million dollars for the property, but his surly sister refused to sell. My dad wanted his share, and it was a long-standing issue between them. When Blake suddenly died, my dad kept it a secret. I didn't find out until two months later.

In a short time my father had managed to clear the house out, and he sold it to the first buyer.

Nobody in my family ever threw anything away. The last time I was there, my deceased grandmother's stockings were still hanging on the towel rack in her bathroom. My dad brought in four gigantic construction-site Dumpsters and loaded them up with free-for-the-taking treasures. He said it was disgusting how all the neighbors went digging through the bins. He complained that they were there day and night; some even jumped right in. I didn't say a word, but I would have been the first to take the plunge. I felt sick thinking about my grandmother's beautiful Nouveau dishes and the elegant silver she had kept wrapped away for special occasions. All the cupboards had been chock-full of amazing vintage textiles. And the pink satin fainting couch, I'd always wanted that fainting couch. I asked my dad, "What did you do with all of Claire's wardrobe?"

The rooms of costumes, all her outrageous hats in their original boxes, the shoe collection from the thirties on. I used to play dress-up in those rooms and daydream of being glamorous. He waved his arm, like "good riddance," and said, "I had the Salvation Army pick all that crap up; you didn't want any of that old stuff, did you?"

I was in total shock. Everything was gone, my heritage dispersed all over Los Angeles. I sighed. "So who bought our house?"

He had to think for a minute. "Oh, some English actor, Julian something."

It couldn't be Julian Sands, could it? I adored him. I saw *A Room with a View* four times; I'd even had a lustful dream about him. I asked, "Was he blond? Is his last name Sands?"

"Yeah, that's it, Julian Sands," he said.

Somehow it made my wearied soul feel a little better. I liked the idea that Julian, my imaginary heartthrob, was living in the house I loved.

16

*P*eddling flowers had been a gentle distraction from my unsteady life, but I was ready for something a bit more challenging. My little son was almost nineteen, and practically out of the house. I hadn't been this free since I was a fourteen-year-old runaway. When my girlfriend Denise Kay suggested we go partners in a vintage clothing store, I jumped right in. We rented a space on trendy Melrose and called our little establishment Two Timer. We decorated the walls in vintage top hats, felt fedoras, and frou-frou ladies' bonnets, and stocked the racks with gentlemen's garb and sequined silky gowns of the past. I was now the proprietor of an actual business. I still sometimes agonized about Joseph, but when he called to say he was remarrying (and not to the soap actress), I was finally convinced the horse was dead.

I met my next and most extraordinary husband when I was with my new partner, Denise, at a Hollywood dinner party. Patrick was the consummate silly Englishman, a one-man Monty Python's Flying Circus.

He'd been successful in the UK as a show host, and now he'd moved across the ocean to California to find his fortune.

Patrick had a disarming boyish charm, but was slightly manic, as if he'd overdosed on sugar cubes. He also drank like a thirsty fish. I gave him my phone number but confided to Denise, "I could never go out with that guy; he'd drive me crazy."

Four years had passed since my hatchet-job marriage to Joseph. I'd had plenty of admirers, but none of them had stood a chance. Not because they weren't attractive or suitable, they simply weren't Joseph. Life was calling me to the banquet, but I refused to go. I preferred to molder away like some heroine in a Jane Austen novel.

There was something different about Patrick that sneaked up on me. He was unthreatening, a charming jester who knew how to make me laugh.

We dated for three months before he felt confident enough to confide in me. There was something important he wanted me to know. Patrick loved the ocean and thought the beach in Santa Monica would be a good place to talk. When we were all cozy, watching the sunset by the pier, I asked him, "Okay, what is it?"

I never would have guessed it in a million, trillion years.

"I like to dress in women's clothes," he confessed.

I thought he was gently trying to tell me he was bisexual, or maybe even homosexual.

"I just like the way women's clothes feel," he said.

I remembered watching a late-night black-and-white movie called *Glen or Glenda*. The film was directed by the eccentric Ed Wood, the master of B movies. Mr. Wood was the scandalous cross-dressing director who Johnny Depp later portrayed in the movie. The funny thing was, I loved that film, and thought Johnny Depp looked smashing in a cashmere tunic. I'd actually bought the video. Little did I know it was a sneak peek into my never-dull destiny, and it was about to become my reality.

"So, you just like to dress in women's clothes, that's all there is to it, nothing weirder? You're not the least bit attracted to men?"

He assured me he wasn't. I was slightly apprehensive, and didn't really get it, but I liked him and it seemed harmless enough. I shrugged my shoulders and said, "All right, then."

Patrick ended up moving in with me, and when his visa was about to expire we rushed a simple church wedding so he could stay in the country. The cross-dressing fetish was pretty interesting. He wasn't garish or flash like a drag queen; quite the contrary. He was most comfortable in a straight skirt with a cardigan and pumps, simple and smart. Patrick had fine features, with big blue eyes and a smooth English complexion. With a touch of mascara and his long brunette hair, he could easily have passed as a tall, lanky girlfriend. I convinced myself that it wasn't a big deal; it was merely a harmless costume.

In the beginning of our marriage, sex with Patrick was strangely arousing. I've always found women sexually attractive but never enough to take the plunge. Being with Patrick was like having a free pass to explore. In female attire he was as pretty and sensuous as any femme fatale, except with boy parts, which made it pretty interesting

Patrick worked hard trying to hit the big time. He got a national commercial, several television pilots, and five nerve-racking callbacks to be a cast member in a popular sitcom. He was always just a bird's breath away from the big time. My store, Two Timer, wasn't making us rich, but it held its own and paid the bills. Before I married Patrick the long hours were fine, but now the shop was like a competing hungry child. When I wasn't manning the counter, I was out trawling swap meets and estate sales for fresh vintage spoils. I was rarely home before nightfall, and my new husband was feeling neglected. We decided to sell the store so I could be a full-time wife and comrade, which suited me fine.

We'd been married just six months when out of the blue I received a call from Diana, my long-lost mother. I'd seen and spoken with her a few times over the years, but mostly kept abreast of her whereabouts through my younger brother, Scot. Years earlier, when I had introduced Diana to her first grandson, she seemed mildly enthusiastic, but when my little tot got fussy and cried, she accused me of overcoddling and spoiling my baby boy. She said that when he whimpered I should put him in a room by himself till he learned to behave. Also, a good spanking on general principles would keep him in line. I decided once again to forgo her and her motherly advice.

Since I'd escaped the fold my mother had given life to two more souls. She'd had a baby girl, Elizabeth, with the folk singer, and six years later a boy, Etienne Saint Laurence, from a fourth marriage. Etienne is four years younger than my own son. I heard that Diana's younger husband had dropped dead from a brain tumor, and that Elizabeth had run away from home at age fourteen. Diana had moved up north to a town called Grass Valley and was raising Etienne, her last child, all on her own. I was surprised to hear from her, but even more stunned when she said she was in Los Angeles and asked if she could stay the night.

It was interesting having my mother as a guest in my own home. She was someone I had quite a history with, but also someone I didn't know at all. The next day I offered to make her an afternoon breakfast, but she opted for three grains of raisin bran, which she ate intently one crumb at a time. She still held fast to her diet of speed, painkillers, cigarettes, and coffee. Unexpectedly, the night turned into two weeks, and I realized Diana was on one of her mystery trips, like the ones she used to take when I was little, only this time it was sixteen-year-old Etienne who was left home alone. The poignant part was that Etienne was about to graduate high school, a considerable achievement in our dysfunctional family. I gently urged my mother to go home and be there for her son's graduation, but she'd become comfortable in my spare room and back in the bustle of Hollywood. A week later my half brother went through the honors with no fanfare or parent present, and my tolerant new husband finally asked, "How long is your mother going to be staying with us?" Having to give anyone the boot can be unpleasant, but it's even more difficult when it's your estranged, willful mother. Another awkward week had passed, when one morning after I finished mopping my kitchen I casually dumped the pail of soapy water down the sink. My mother, who had taken to following me around the house, gave me a look of horror and disbelief. In her familiar, dominant tone, she asked, "Catherine, why did you just waste that perfectly good water?"

For a brief moment I was flustered without a reasonable excuse. I'd zoomed right back to 1960, when I was ten years old. I'd forgotten: In her house we saved and reused soapy water till it was black with dirt. In forty years I'd never once been defiant, questioned, or spoken back to Diana, but she was waiting for my reply. I felt slightly faint, then boldly piped, "If this was your house I would have saved it, but this is my house. I can pour the whole pail down the drain if I like."

There was an odd pause; she cocked her head with a puzzled expression, and said, "I guess you're right." I took that opportunity to tell her, "Mother, it's time for you to go back home."

The first year with Patrick was marital bliss, but when the cash ran low I needed to find employment. I'd just turned forty and had little formal education. My major was in creativity, with an A in survival.

It was coming on Christmas, and three blocks away on the corner of Franklin and La Brea was a bustling Christmas tree lot. I suggested to Patrick that we go over and see if we could get a part-time position selling trees for some extra Christmas cash. The proprietor was as friendly as Santa and hired us on the spot. Patrick did most of the heavy work, but I was pretty good at enchanting the customers, and was having good fun learning to flock the pines. The week before Christmas the owner of the lot said he had to get back to Laguna Beach, and asked if we wanted to take over the whole shebang. He said we could keep half of everything we sold, and could even use his little trailer to keep warm in. All of a sudden Patrick and I were running a tree business and had giant wads of cold cash, and I do mean cold. We were freezing our butts off. Every chance we got we'd huddle in the trailer to get away from the winter wind. I brought along festive bottles of Bailey's to stave off the chill. By the end of the chilly nights we were like a pair of tipsy elves. The night before Christmas we had earned four thousand dollars, which meant two thousand was ours to keep. Before closing the lot and pulling the plug on the colored lights we picked the biggest, most majestic of the leftover Noble firs, and the two of us carried the piny-scented tree all the way home.

Still chasing our elusive fortune, I said to my English husband, "I bet I could get a job photo doubling for Diane Keaton, or maybe I could write a book about my curious life."

Patrick teased me, "Are you a writer now? I didn't know you knew Diane Keaton."

I wasn't, and didn't, but ever since the movie *Annie Hall* debuted, I was often mistaken for Diane, and I had heard she was about to start a new picture.

I looked up her agent at William Morris and submitted a few Polaroids, along with my phone number and a little note requesting to work on her next film. I never did get a reply, but as luck would have it, my old friend, serendipity, was waiting in the wings.

Patrick and I were at a Hollywood soiree when a casting agent approached me, exclaiming, "You look so much like Diane Keaton. I'm casting a movie with her, and you'd be a great stand-in and photo double for her."

At the interview, for a prank, the producer introduced me to the writer and director of photography as Diane. They didn't even question it. They shook my hand and said, "Nice to meet you, Diane."

I got the job, and ended up working on two more films with her. I traveled to New York, San Francisco, and the Hamptons with Diane, and at the end of each film she gave me a personal cash bonus, along with divine books on photography. At the end of the last movie, *Town and Country*, she read the first chapter of my book and encouraged me, "Keep writing, Catherine."

I always think how amazing it is that a single thought can open the universe and lead you on amazing adventures.

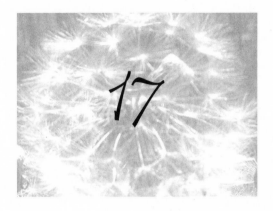

At 3:00 A.M. Patrick and I were awakened from a deep sleep. It was my dad on the telephone, weeping, "Loren isn't breathing, I think she's dead!"

By the time the paramedics arrived Loren had clearly departed. At age fifty-five she had looked pretty spry to me, but apparently she had just stopped breathing in her sleep.

I'd never really gotten to spend much intimate time with my father, mainly because Loren, my stepmother, harbored a deranged jealousy toward me. She behaved like I was "the other woman" trying to horn in on her territory, and she never missed an opportunity to be rude or insulting. The last time we spoke she sweetly said, "Your father's a very busy man. When he has free time he spends it with me, do you understand?"

Calling their house was a guaranteed slap in the face, and I eventually gave up. Her mysterious demise left me the last surviving James, and the only one my dad had left. I was hoping it would give us a chance to be closer, and that perhaps I would at last have a father.

I should have been more careful what I asked for. After the funeral I became his sole lifeline. He'd call at all hours, irrational and incoherent. In a pool of moonshine, he'd slur, "You have to come over right now, I don't think I'm going to make it."

I'd race over the hill to Studio City, only to find my father passed out cold on his leather sofa. His hair would be awry, and an empty quart of Gentleman Jack lay by his side. So this was my dad, the man I'd fantasized about all these years; he was a full-on alcoholic maniac. I gently laid a comforter over him and tiptoed out the door.

I was surprised at how quickly he recovered from Loren's departure. Within a month he had sold his home of twenty years and picked up and moved to Palm Springs.

The distance was actually a relief. There wouldn't be any more late-night calls or emergency excursions to the valley; hopefully he'd be happier in the dunes of the desert. Sadly, the calls soon got more desperate. He was lonely and hated it there. My dad wreaked havoc and caused commotion everywhere he went. He'd been kicked out of all the local bars and bistros, and had been arrested twice for drunk and disorderly conduct. He had also been involved in two drunken traffic accidents in the first month. My poor old dad was out of control.

Patrick and I decided we'd better go check on him, and packed our bags for what would be one wacky weekend.

We assumed he'd be alone, and that we'd take him out for a little dinner, maybe see a movie, try to cheer him up a bit. When we arrived, a party was already under way. He'd invited a few of his closest drinking chums to meet us. The whole lot of them were already pummeled and staggering about at the crack of noon.

My dad took us aside and murmured, "I told my friends you were both in your twenties, so if anyone asks, just say you're twenty-four."

Patrick and I grimaced. At forty-one I still looked youthful, but certainly not twenty-four. One of his cronies slurred, "Oh, how nice, you kids are the same age as my daughter; you two have to get together."

When we politely turned down an invitation for afternoon cocktails the old sots adjourned to a more private party in the den, leaving my husband and me alone in the living room. We felt like uninvited guests, and I was slightly embarrassed. I whispered to Patrick, "Should we just get out of here?"

We were about to make our excuses when my dad announced, "Okay, kids, we're all going to lunch."

To our dismay, we were roped in for the all-night duration.

After a long rough day of drinking, and several Vicodins later, my weary dad was ready to hit the hay, and he passed out by 8:00 P.M. With nothing much else to do in the desert, Patrick and I headed for the guestroom with the stubborn sofa bed.

No matter how hard we tugged and pulled, the bed would only open three fourths of the way out. We jumped on it, tried to prop it up with the end tables, and basically wrestled ourselves into a sweaty exhaustion. We finally fell asleep with our heads at the foot of the bed on a thirty-degree tilt, like Frankenstein on the slab.

My father was an early riser, always up and at 'em by 4:00 A.M. In his eyes, if you slept past five you were a derelict. By 6:00 A.M., when Patrick and I were still in slumber, my dad was about to explode with fury. Using his elaborate stereo system, he blasted us awake by an ear-piercing volley of nose-diving fighter planes, with bombs bursting in air, followed by Tchaikovsky's "1812 Overture." We didn't know whether to charge or run for cover.

My dad had already eaten his breakfast and was busy setting up his portable bar for the day. He systematically set out a fresh bucket of ice, a full quart of Jack, a liter of Diet Coke, and an empty Vicodin bottle for measuring shots. He was ready to meet the day. He pulled out a bundle of Polaroids and shouted, "Hey kids, I want to show you some pictures of a friend of mine."

He handed me a stack of some pretty bizarre photographs. At first glance I thought, "This is the single most unattractive woman I'd ever laid eyes on." I gently inquired, "Oh, is this one of your girlfriends?"

With an elated grin he said, "No, she's just a good friend."

Something strange was going on. I shuffled through the pictures a few times before realizing they were all of him, my dad in drag. The rings he was wearing were identical to those in the photographs. Was my father a cross-dresser too?

"She looks like a pretty tall girl."

He modestly replied, "Yes, she's a showgirl from Vegas."

I've heard that girls look for qualities similar to their fathers' when choosing a husband, but I hardly knew my dad. Was the universe trying to tell me something? How could it be that the two men in my life were both alcoholic powder girls?

In the passing weeks I received a myriad of wild calls that got stranger by the day. One day my dad said he'd been arrested and was calling from jail. I asked him, "What jail?" and said that I'd come to get him, but all of a sudden he couldn't talk any longer. He said the guard was making him hang the phone up. Next he said he'd sold his house, moved to South America, and was living in a trailer in the jungle. Later that week he was flying a Cessna over the desert, and it was running out of fuel. He said he was about to crash and wanted to tell me he loved me before the plane went down; then the phone went dead. I could hear the roar of the plane engines in the background, so I believed he was flying. That time he actually scared me, but there wasn't a lot I could do. I'd heard so many of his insane tales in the past and prayed, "Please let it be another one of his crazy stories." Of course he was fine and didn't remember anything about the in-flight phone call the next day.

When he called saying he had prostate cancer and had to have his penis removed, I humored him with, "Yikes, that sounds a little extreme; have you gotten a second opinion?"

He said he'd seen several doctors, and they all agreed it would have to come off.

Besides being an incorrigible drama merchant, my dad was a habitual hypochondriac. Over time I'd become numb to his absurd tales and bizarre antics for attention. But he said he was leaving in the morning and actually gave me the phone number of a hospital in Colorado. I wondered, was it real this time?

I doubted there was any truth to the latest yarn, but my curiosity finally got the better of me. I called the number he had given me just to check. Holy shit, it was a real hospital, and he was actually a registered patient. Up till now I'd been coolly blasé, but suddenly I felt sick to my stomach.

I asked the receptionist to please connect me to his room. A male nurse answered his phone and informed me, "She's just come out of the operation. The surgery went well, but she's still a little groggy,"

She? "I'm sorry," I said, "I must have the wrong room. I'm looking for Mr. Robert James, my father, he's a *man*."

The male RN replied, "You have the right room, hon. Why don't you call back a little later, when she's more alert."

I dropped the receiver like a hot coal. It was worse than cancer; he'd been mutilated! As if he wasn't confused enough, now he was a man-made woman. Maybe I didn't understand the nurse right; this had to be a mistake. I called back later and my dad answered the phone. In a caring tone, I said, "I called you earlier and spoke with a nurse. What kind of operation did you have?" My father sounded dazed and said he'd call me in a few days, when he got back home.

That first luncheon fiasco at Musso's was like falling into a bramble of thorns. I'd accepted that my father was essentially unsound, but now that he wasn't even a man anymore, he felt and looked like a downright stranger! It wasn't just the physical aspect; he'd taken on a whole new persona; he behaved coy and coquettish. During our lunch he delighted in speaking to me about intimate feminine details, as if I was a close girlfriend. I didn't want to talk to my father about feminine hygiene, hormonal mood swings, or lipstick shades. I don't think it ever occurred to him how it affected me, or my weary brain. I felt like my synapses were buckling, refusing to connect. Nevertheless, he was the man who had given me life, and I did my best to be a supportive daughter.

Whenever he came to town we made arrangements to meet for lunch, then we'd go to Forest Lawn to put fresh flowers on Loren's grave. He always showed up in full fright drag. I'd lag behind in astonishment as he maneuvered the grassy hillside of the cemetery in his unsteady high-heeled gait and tight-fitting skirt. He looked about as graceful as a wounded bat.

On Robin's sixty-third birthday Patrick was working in England, so I enlisted my pretty blond girlfriend Sandra to accompany me to Palm Springs for a little celebration. Sandra wasn't a girl who was easily fazed, and she possessed a wicked sense of humor, so she'd be the perfect companion for the weekend pilgrimage. I filled her in on my dad's eccentricities and she assured me she could handle it.

We suited up for the unexpected, and tapped on his/her front door. I expected to see a bewigged Aunt Bea, but my dad was dressed like a man, in crisp tennis whites, with just a hint of lip rouge. The only real giveaways were his copious, unbridled boobs, which were stretching his polo shirt to the limit. He was already a bit tipsy but doing his best to be a gracious host. He leaned over and whispered, "I didn't want to embarrass you."

He then lost his balance and toppled into us, knocking all three of us to the ground. Sandra and I scrambled to our feet, but my dad was down for the count, still tangled in the lamp cord and room divider that collapsed when he tried to steady himself. The look on Sandra's face was priceless, and this was just the first thirty seconds of a long, looming weekend. I could see that she didn't know whether to laugh or run for the desert. We gave my dad a hand up, and as if nothing had happened, he asked, "Hey, would you kids like to go for a swim?"

My dad's desert home was a suburban three-bedroom tract house in the center of Rancho Mirage. He had a lovely manicured garden with wrought-iron love seats, a birdbath, and an inviting swimming pool. The interior was adorned with sentimental china, Italian scenic oils, and pots of dried flower arrangements. The only hint of manliness was his extensive stereo equipment, theater-sized television set, and his fire engine–red Ferrari parked in the garage.

We were already in the pool when my dad came out resembling the Creature from the Black Lagoon. In the 120-degree desert heat, he was clad in a full, antiquated deep-sea diving suit, ready to swim some laps. If he wasn't such a loon, he would have made quite the comedian.

After dinner my dad suggested we go for a moonlit dip in the Jacuzzi, and he disappeared into the garden to turn the thing on. I don't know what happened, but ten minutes later he stumbled back into the house with a bleeding gash on his forehead and scraped bloody grass stains on both knees. I blurted out, "Oh my God, you're bleeding!"

He said it was nothing, but he was bleeding pretty badly. I sat him down, bandaged his wounds, and cleaned the grass stains off his knees. This man was a walking accident; I wondered how he made it through a day. We decided to forgo the Jacuzzi and opted for a nice safe movie from Blockbuster. Sandra said she had heard *The Crying Game* was really good, so that's what my dad rented. Fortunately we were only a third into the film when my dad, who was sauced to the gills, decided to hit the sack. When I realized the transsexual plot, I almost fainted. I whispered to Sandra, "How could you have suggested this video?"

She swore she didn't have a clue.

In the midst of my dad's drama in the desert, I received a call from my mother in the foothills of Grass Valley. Etienne had left home and moved in with my brother Scot; meanwhile my sister, Elizabeth, had gotten into trouble with drugs, and was remanded to a rehab facility somewhere in Nevada. Like myself, Elizabeth had also had a baby in her teens. It seems that when my sister was growing up our mother used me as the faultless weapon. I was the mysterious sister, the model and singer who lived in England with rock-and-roll legends. She held me over Elizabeth's head as the shining example. "Why couldn't you have been more like Catherine?"

Elizabeth did the next best thing. Her baby was born on my birthday, and Elizabeth named her new daughter Catherine.

While my young sister was being rehabilitated, Diana somehow gained custody of eight-year-old Catherine, and history was being repeated.

I had hoped that maybe the years had softened Diana, but after the first phone call I realized that as long as my mother had a heartbeat there wasn't a chance in China. Diana confided to me that Catherine was an evil girl who needed to be punished. I said to my mother, "That's what you used to say about me. How bad can she be, she's just a child." I tried to tell my mother that having a new Catherine with my same birthday was like a fresh chance to amend the past, but she wouldn't hear me. Knowing young Catherine's dismal destiny, I wrote letters, sent cards, and tried to call, but Catherine was always on restriction or unavailable. I later learned that Catherine had shared my same fate with her grandmother. Besides living at the foot of terror, there was also the same diet regimen, little food, plenty of Tabasco, and Dawn dishwashing liquid to wash it down with. Catherine also told me that Diana had twisted her arm so hard that it broke. I decided then that there was no reason to ever see or speak with my mother again.

Patrick kept extending his trip in England, till he finally got up the courage to tell me he didn't want to come back to America at all. He said it was too hot and sweaty for him in California, and he missed his family and friends. I loved Patrick, but we'd become more like pals than husband and wife; maybe it was best he didn't come home.

In the fourteen years I lived on El Cerrito Place, I grieved the loss of my boyfriend Paul, trudged through the wreckage of my marriage to Joseph, and raised a healthy son who was now married and had his own baby son. With all that enlightenment under my belt, Patrick's departure was not quite as painful as in the past. It seemed simply that our time together was up. At forty-three I was back on my own and ready to turn the page.

I'd been dreaming about going to New York, maybe even going back to Connecticut. I missed the seasons, the turning of the leaves, the snow, the adventure of it all. At twenty-three I would have jumped on a plane and not looked back, but now for some reason it felt a little more complicated.

My lifelong friend Patti D'Arbanville, whom I had met in Greenwich Village when I was fourteen, had become a successful actress, married a handsome fireman, and moved to the picturesque town of Sea Cliff, New York. I had a standing invitation to come for a visit and decided to take her up on it.

So I took a deep breath and packed up fourteen years of memories and crapola and deposited them in a storage vault on the corner of Franklin and Vine.

Patti's home was a cozy three-story eight-bedroom Victorian abode. The place took up an entire block, complete with a surrounding white picket fence and a Catholic church the next lot over. Her street was wide and lined with regal elms and oaks, and rambling historical houses set far back from the road. I expected to see Andy Hardy coming around the corner at any moment.

Patti had just procured the role of Lieutenant Cooper on the Fox cop show *New York Undercover,* and graciously managed to wangle me in as her stand-in. I'm a full four inches taller than she is, but it didn't seem to matter; we were together again, and I was gainfully employed in New York City.

It had been two decades since I'd left my cottage in Connecticut. For twenty years I had had recurring dreams of going back there, but in my dreams someone else was living in my house. Sometimes I dreamed it had been abandoned and I'd secretly moved back in. Now was my chance; I was going back for real.

I boarded the train at Grand Central and rode a taxi from the familiar Brewster station to my beloved Candlewoood Lake. What a shock! The formerly rural Route 7 was now built up and besmirched to the point of being almost unrecognizable. My quaint little Carvel ice cream stand was now a shopping strip. In place of the graceful weeping willows and grand maples stood bright-colored fast-food chains littering the pastoral landscape. But once I turned up onto the lush, green Huckleberry Hill, I knew I'd arrived. I wondered for a moment, "Is this real, or just another one of my wishful dreams?" I passed the two dips in the road where the Pontiac would take to the air and fly like a bird, and it all came back. Just a little farther and I'd be at the lake.

Ah, there it was, this was the spot, but my cottage was gone! Only the burned-out, weathered remnants of my stone fireplace, front porch, and blistered window frames remained. There were wild blackberries twisting through the charred window sashes, and winding around the granite fireplace, almost in celebration. I pushed back what was left of the scorched window casing and was startled to see an uncharred strip of clear plastic neatly stapled close to the hinges in the wood. It was the very plastic I'd put up over twenty years earlier to keep the cold wind out. An amazing feeling came over me. It wasn't just a mysterious burned-down house. I knew its history. I knew that girl, the girl and her blond baby boy who once lived here.

It was early October, and the lake had the same peaceful lull I'd fallen in love with. There was a faint breeze in the air, and the shimmering leaves were beginning to turn color and fall to the ground. I could hear the gentle sound of the lake lapping the shore and wild geese flapping their feathers, ready to migrate south for the winter. I lay back on what was left of the surrounding stone wall and breathed it all in, inhaling the moment, all the sweet memories of me and my son, both of us growing up here.

I was lost in the rapture of it all when I heard distant voices coming up from the lake. It was an elderly couple walking hand-in-hand, relishing the last weeks of fall. As they neared me, I asked, "Excuse me, do you know what happened to this house? When did it burn down?"

The woman answered, "Oh, the place burned down years ago. There was a girl with a child who used to live here. When they left, her boyfriend came back and set it on fire."

Oh, my God, was it Chris? Did he really burn the place down to the ground? I knew he'd be upset when he found me gone, but I didn't think he possessed that level of rage. I could just imagine him dowsing the cherry logs with gasoline, then reveling in his fury as the old place went up in a blaze.

I suddenly realized that the couple I was speaking to were my former summer neighbors from up the road, Mr. and Mrs. Sobel. In just twenty years they'd gone from older to elderly. They seemed happy to see me again and invited me to their cottage for a nice cup of tea and an update on the history of the lake.

I thought it odd that in all these years no one had ever rebuilt on my premium property, but was thankful to be able to see my beautiful little spot one more time, even in its charred, overgrown glory.

Miss Pamela was in New York to research and write a chapter for her latest book, *Rock Bottom*. Her subject was the scandalous, dearly departed GG Allin. GG was the punk rocker who shocked and disgusted his spectators by defecating on stage, sometimes hurling his putrid poop into the audience or eating his own excrement. Pamela showed me a video of him performing at New York University, where even the hardest-core rockers ran for cover.

She casually mentioned that Led Zeppelin was in town to be inducted into the Rock and Roll Hall of Fame at Radio City Music Hall, and she wanted to go to the party. She asked if I'd call Jimmy Page so we could go. Call Jimmy? I hadn't seen him in over ten years, nor did I have a clue where he was staying. She said he was at the Essex House on Central Park, but didn't know the secret password to get through to his room. I was hesitant to call. Such a long time had passed, but I eventually relented and tried the moniker he had used twenty years ago. I was sure the hotel operator would tell me nobody was registered by that title, but then I heard Jimmy's unmistakable, angelic, soft voice. After all these years it still made my heart patter.

"Hello, Jimmy, this is Catherine."

It was like we'd spoken yesterday. When I told him I was in New York he was excited, and said, "Come over right now, let's have dinner, anywhere you would like."

We met at his hotel on Central Park West, and what a surprise. In my memory he was still the velvet-clad, lithesome prince with soft long ringlets and a majestic air, but something amazing had happened: We had both gotten older. It was like a veil had lifted. It was still us, we still had the history, but it wasn't quite so mysterious; it felt more comfortable, and at ease.

Arm-in-arm, we window shopped along Central Park like old friends and reminisced of our feral youthful days. It was almost a relief, the painful passion, the burning torch I'd carted around all these years had smoldered into a cinder, or so I thought.

In the soft romantic light of the Plaza Hotel and two Cosmopolitans later, Jimmy began to look exactly as he had the day we met—still dangerous. There's something about one's eyes that never change. I got that same old achy feeling, the one that goes right through your soul. After dinner we were touring around the Plaza, when Jimmy grabbed me and said, "Why don't we just run away together right now; we could go anywhere."

As always, he disarmed me completely, but I dismissed the offer with a giggle.

"Well, then," he said, "if you don't want to run away with me, would you at least be my date for the Hall of Fame induction?"

I felt bad breaking the news to Miss Pamela, but I was going, and that was that. It seemed kind of perfect that I would be his girl on this grand occasion.

Before meeting up with Robert Plant and John Paul Jones in the downstairs hotel lounge, I helped Jimmy with his impossible bow tie, which neither of us had a clue how to tie. It was the first time I'd ever seen Mr. Page in a tux. Yes, we'd definitely grown up.

The limo was waiting and the revelry was about to begin. I had had no idea what a big deal this was. Besides Led Zeppelin there were also Neil Young, the Allman Brothers, and the transcendent Al Green, whom I worship and adore, all being inducted that night.

Al Green opened the ceremony with "Take Me to the River," and left me longing for more with "Love and Happiness." After a grand dinner and several long-winded speeches, Jimmy got up and jammed with Neil Young, and I was gone like a rocket, transported right back to 1968.

When Jimmy went onstage a young man had taken his seat at our table and tried to chat me up. When Jimmy came offstage he strolled up and announced to the swain, "Number nine, your time is up."

And the would-be beau scurried off in a huff. Ha! After all these years, Jimmy still had a jealous streak for me.

We rode the limo back to the hotel, and I thought, "This is all happening pretty fast. Oh well, I'll think about it later." When we got to his room, we kissed like the gods. No one has ever kissed me the way Jimmy did. He inhaled my breath, still stealing my soul; I could almost see the misty vapors passing between us. His breath and taste were still sweet as a baby's, and as hot as high-voltage wire, but I couldn't get into the moment. The imps and angels were looming in my head, spryly clattering, "Do you really want to start this? He's off to London in the morning." Nope, I wasn't up for another potential heartache, but it sure felt dreamy. He could feel my vacillating doubt and whispered in his softest voice, "What do you want, my girl?"

It was five in the morning, and I didn't know.

With a smile, I replied, "I think I better go before the sun comes up."

We got dressed, and he walked me down to the waiting limo. I blew kisses until we turned the block, and that's the last time I saw the ever-dazzling Mr. Page.

L iving in Sea Cliff, staying with Patti, was more than comfy, but I was beginning to feel a bit like the spinster aunt up on the third floor. She had a family, three babies, and a firefighter husband to look after. I missed having my own kitchen, my own things, and time alone. It was time to go home, back to California.

I'd saved a bit of money working with Patti on *New York Undercover*, but unfortunately it wouldn't sustain me for long. The rentals in Los Angeles had soared, and I had to settle on a smallish place in the flat-lands of Hollywood.

At first glance, the 1930s duplex on Curson Avenue appeared to have some charm, but unfortunately it had been remodeled in the late seventies. The lovely old vaulted ceilings had been desecrated with cottage cheese, and updated with whirling chrome ceiling fans. The kitchen was stippled in black, and the whole muddle was topped off with black-and-white vertical disco shades. I checked under the shag carpeting and, lucky for me, the original hardwood floors were still intact. It would be some work, but it seemed like a quiet neighborhood, and I was desperate for a spot of sanctuary, a key to my own front door. With some spit and polish, a few plumes and tassels, I could turn a closet into a palace.

The first cozy night I was industriously scraping the cheese from the ceiling when I heard a stir of ouds and percussion instruments. The loud din overtook my new abode, completely drowning out my heavenly Mozart. In the morning I awoke to the sound of a spitting pressure cooker wafting a pungent aroma of pork, onions, cilantro, and garlic that permeated my entire apartment. I heard a clamor of shrill, Farsi-speaking voices, and peeked out my disco shades to see what the commotion was about. There they were, my new neighbors, dressed in heavy veils and hanging chunks of animal flesh off metal hooks in the backyard. With my freshly signed lease it looked like I'd be spending an aromatic year in little Iran.

I was down to my last three hundred dollars, and just in the nick of time I found employment working on scale models for the new Jurassic Park ride at Universal Studios. Before I met my husband Joseph, I had worked for a company called Landmark Entertainment. I did scenic painting for the King Kong ride at Universal's theme park and designed props for the Busch Gardens attractions. I called my old boss at Landmark and he hired me over the phone.

I'd work all day, then come home and rip up heaps of sullied gold-shag carpeting, lugging the remnants down the stairs to the garbage. I wondered, "How did my life get down to this?"

My new job became a lot more interesting when a whimsical show designer arrived in my department. He looked like a young Robert Redford, with mischievous blue eyes and a blinding smile. I started getting up a half hour early just to get extra dolled up for work.

Ovid Pope was a forty-two-year-old teenager with a wondrous sense of adventure and a shared love of natural beauty.

On our first date he wowed me with his wondrous artwork. There was one particular piece he called "The Dancing Fairies." It was a ring of tiny delicate fairies with flickering wings that looked real. They jumped, flew, and bowed in continues circular motion. I'd never seen anything so beautiful. He later took me hiking by his house in the hills of Silver Lake, introducing me to ancient macadamia trees and fields of purple lupine. I smelled the essence of native sage crushed from his fingertips, and we lunched on wild pomegranates while sitting on a bluff overlooking the balmy glen. While watching him divide the crimson red pomegranate with his Boy Scout pocketknife, I thought, "This is my kind of man."

In three short months I had found a new boyfriend and inspiring employment, and turned my Hollywood apartment into a shabby chic haven. I'd become accustomed to my neighbors' resonant Eastern music recitals, and even gotten used to the persistent scent of garlic wafting up through my windows. But when summer arrived my apartment was like an Indian sweat lodge. While fanning myself in front of my fridge to cool off, I thought, "What I really need is a place with central air, and a nice cool pool."

A month earlier, Heather and Roger Daltrey had been visiting Los Angeles and stayed at a stunning mountaintop home in Beverly Hills. The retreat sat on the tip-top of a secluded private drive, and from the back garden swimming pool there was a clear view of downtown Los Angeles, all the way to Catalina Island. I remember thinking, "Wow, I would just love to live here."

The estate belonged to John Paul DeJoria, chief and ruler of the renowned Paul Mitchell Systems hair products. As it turned out, his former property manager had recently taken leave, and he was looking for a replacement. I didn't know it at the time, but Roger had recommended me for the position. When John Paul's wife, the Southern blond beauty Eloise, called to ask if I'd be interested in the job, I was amazed. It was just yesterday that I had asked the heavens for a place with a pool, and here it was. My job was coordinating the workers and gardeners, and to arrange fresh flowers when guests came to visit. The position included the upstairs residence, with full use of the pool and wooded gardens. John Paul handed me the keys to his home, and I didn't see or speak with him again till the holidays, when I received an invitation to his annual Christmas party. It was actually more than a mere party; it was an extravagant Renaissance costume ball held at his Malibu fortress. I procured a vintage Elizabethan gown, and after adjusting the plume in my bonnet and stuffing the billowing hoop-skirt and petticoats into the front seat of my car, I was off to the palace.

The whimsical cast of Cirque du Soleil were performing in the manicured gardens, and they greeted the guests in their ethereal style. Wolfgang Puck, clad in chef whites, presided over an elegant spread of Christmas delicacies, and Rod Stewart had taken the stage in the main room. I've been to some pretty amazing places in my life, but this night was one of the grandest.

The most extraordinary part of taking care of John Paul's Beverly Hills estate was that not a soul lived in the house except me. Once or twice a year, one of the DeJorias' celebrated friends would camp out for a few days, but otherwise I had the entire hill completely to myself. Besides the generous annual invitations, John Paul also supplied me with cases of his luxurious Paul Mitchell conditioners, sprays, and more shampoo than I could lather up in a lifetime. Knowing John Paul was like having my own angel. Living in his hilltop heaven allowed me the time to think of what I really wanted to do. It was in this stunning little eagle's nest that I found the inspiration and had the opportunity to begin writing.

I hadn't spoken with my father since I had gotten back to California. Now that I'd settled in, I thought it would be nice to invite him up to my grand new quarters for Thanksgiving. Over the next month I left several messages, but then got a recording saying his number had been disconnected. That's weird, I thought. Where the heck was he? I had his attorney's number; surely he'd know where to find him. I'd always thought my dad's lawyer was a bit of a joker but had had no idea to what depths he would descend.

I called and asked,

"Hello, Mr. S. My dad's number has been disconnected, do you know where he is? Has he moved?"

Mr. S. seemed uncomfortable and stiffly replied, "Your father is dead."

Oh my God, my heart started to thump out of my chest.

"When did he die?"

"About two months ago."

Then there was silence; I was utterly stunned. "Why didn't anyone call me?"

He said he didn't have my number, although it was listed. I had so many questions.

"Where did he die? What from? When was his funeral? Was he buried as a Mason, as he'd requested?"

S. said he had died in the hospital from sepsis. I asked if he'd been on life support, and the attorney said my father had declined it.

I started to ask questions: "Why were you at the hospital in Palm Springs? What about Dad's belongings? His home in Rancho Mirage?" I wanted to go down there. S. stopped me short, telling me that my father's property belonged to him and his wife now, that my father left everything to his wife in his will.

Was he insane? I'd seen my father's will; I knew where he kept it. As I was his daughter and only acknowledged survivor, he'd left his entire estate to me. I'd even gone with him to this lawyer's office when he signed the document. I asked, "So you're saying I can't even go to my father's house?"

"That's right." He seemed to gloat, but told me that he had saved some of the family photo albums if I wanted them.

Besides the shock of learning that my father was dead, I couldn't believe what I was hearing. I inquired, "What about my dad's model airplane collection?"

"Yeah, I think they're still hanging up; you can have 'em." This guy was dead serious; I was about to be screwed. I asked, "Should I get my own counsel?"

"I can't advise you of that," he muttered. "It's up to you; but you've been left ten percent of the residue. I should tell you, however, there's a clause in the will that states that if you try to contest it, you lose your ten percent and only get one dollar."

I had to ask, "Did you draft this will?"

But of course he had.

With all the Vicodin abuse and years of boozing, my poor old dad was an easy mark, and I imagine young Mr. S. was counting on the apple not falling far from the tree. He probably assumed I was some powerless hippie-dippy from Hollywood, an aimless airhead without a clue about how to defend myself, but he was so wrong. I'd already been cheated out of a childhood, a family, and an education. I wasn't about to let a stranger take away my inheritance as well.

At 8:00 A.M. I was at the Riverside County Courthouse, poring over my dad's last will and testament. Not only had the new will left everything to Mrs. S., there was also a bequest of twenty thousand dollars to S.'s mother-in-law. His wife's mother! I assumed my father had never even met her! The pièce de résistance was my father's signature on the will. To me it looked like a clear forgery, but how was I going to prove it? There were some other interesting documents as well. I noticed that S. had filed papers the day my father died, giving his wife access to my dad's property and bank accounts. I needed an attorney fast.

I employed Ovid, my new beau, to take a little trip with me down to Palm Springs. I was going to my father's home, whether S. liked it or not, and I wasn't a day too soon. My dad's belongings had been picked over and cleaned out. There were two twenty-foot Dumpsters outside the house, overflowing with a life's worth of possessions.

Ovid gave me a boost up, and I fell into the tangled heap of discarded memories. It seemed so tragic, but every now and then I'd dig up a little treasure that made the Dumpster dive worth it. My heart felt sick when I found a crumpled duffel bag containing my dad's cherished racing coveralls. I later found his crash helmet, with his name and gold wings flanking the sides. I remembered my dad being quite a handsome sight in his racing gear. I found the rosary I'd given him last Christmas, and the only surviving picture of my grandparents. There were loads of family photos, including one of me that he had kept on his nightstand, but the glass had been smashed in the jumble. I dug my way to the bottom and was saddened to find the shattered plastic remains of my dad's fragile World War II model planes that he'd assembled and painted when he was just a boy. How in God's name had my father let this man into his life? Now I was left to deal with this appalling situation.

I met with several lawyers, thinking my case was an obvious slam dunk and clearly unjust, but nobody would touch it without a ten-thousand-dollar retainer. It occurred to me that it was just what the opposition was counting on. Plus, it seemed attorneys don't like to do battle with their own. There was also the huge matter of a document called a Certificate of Independent Review, which S. claimed to have in his possession. A Certificate of Independent Review was put into law to stop unscrupulous attorneys from taking advantage of elderly, incapacitated clients. If a client wanted to leave a gift of cash or property to their attorney, their will would have to be independently reviewed and signed by a separate, nonaffiliated law office in order to make the gift valid. Most attorneys steer clear of gifts even to their spouses, as it tends to put them in an unfavorable spotlight.

I tracked down the lawyer who allegedly reviewed my father's last testament. He had a questionable history. He'd been suspended from the bar twice, and had two long pages of fraud complaints. Things were looking up. If he hadn't reviewed the will, S. didn't stand a chance. Even if he had, his integrity could be challenged. After several unanswered calls, the snake finally surfaced and said he had no recall of meeting with my father, even when told he was a transsexual, a character not easily forgotten. My dad would have shown up in full drag, as the document was made out in his female alias. The story was getting cheesier by the second. Meanwhile, S. had closed my dad's bank accounts and was readying his home for sale.

I found an estate lawyer in Palms Springs who was highly amused with my story and agreed to take my case on for a five-thousand-dollar retainer and 33 percent of the estate or 40 percent if we went to trial. It felt like highway robbery, but time was running out. I wasn't about to let a stranger outrageously rob me.

I called Roger Daltrey in England and told him of my predicament, and without a question, he FedExed me a check for five thousand the very next day.

The lawyer I hired had practiced probate law for almost fifty years and seemed pretty well versed. Unfortunately, he wasn't exactly a pit bull in this arena. On my request, he did have the will analyzed for forgery, and according to the specialist, the signature was fraudulent. My lawyer's forte was estate planning, not criminal investigation. I ended up doing all the legwork, and he filed the legal documents.

In the beginning S. didn't take me seriously; he was pompous and smug and refused to hand over any financial accounts of my father's estate. Eventually, we got access to some records. As it turned out, S. had deposited some of the money into accounts he could access. And he was tooling around in my dad's Cobra! He was even paying his legal expenses with money from the estate.

It had been an arduous year, but my judicial efforts hadn't been in vain. I was about to have my day in the courtroom.

My old comrades Patti D'Arbanville and Miss Pamela rallied to my cause. Patti, who flew in from New York, and Pamela, who had just had her face cosmetically lasered to raw pulp, were coming to give testimony.

We opted to ride in Ovid's Volvo station wagon, thinking it would be more spacious for the journey, but halfway through the scorching desert, the air conditioner conked out. It was 113 degrees in the shade, and Miss Pamela's poor face was as red as a sliced tomato. She had it saturated in antibiotic ointment, and it looked like it was about to melt. We sang every Beatles song we knew to keep our brains off the blistering heat, but there was no comfort in sight, just miles of barren, blanched landscape.

When we got to our hotel all four of us jumped in the pool like a pack of giddy teenagers; we had made it!

The trial was hanging heavily over my head. I'd explored and researched every avenue I could think of. There was no way I wouldn't win, but what if I lost? I tried to look on the bright side; I'd been given a free crash course in probate law and had gotten pretty proficient in math. It was like a wily game of chess, merely a matter of who did their homework, who played the better game, and who knew how best to slip through the slippery loopholes. It was a separate, exact language only to be defined in the *Black's Law Dictionary*; there was nothing fair or just about it.

My attorney was an admirable, decent chap, but he was getting on in age and I wasn't sure he was tough enough to stand up to the squirrelly resistance. I assumed S. was a dirty fighter and would go in for the kill. Walking into the courtroom, seeing the assemblage of somber suits, I had an amazing epiphany. With my incessant perseverance, I had single-handedly created this moment. All these strangers had gotten out of bed this morning and were in this courtroom because I was alive. As seemingly impossible as it was, I had made it happen.

First up was the question of the independent review. The lawyer in question had no recollection, notes, or payment in regards to his supposed meeting with my father, nor did he recognize the many photos he was shown. He did remember that it was his birthday and that he was out of town on that date. He was in a sticky position. He agreed it was his signature on the document, but if he hadn't met with my dad, which he clearly had not, he could face being disbarred. He ended his testimony saying, "As it is my signature, I must have performed the review."

During his testimony I frantically scribbled notes to my attorney with questions I wanted him to ask in his cross-examination. This was the crux of my case; I wanted it to be categorically clear that he and my father had never met, but he shushed me away, whispering, "I know what I'm doing."

I was bursting with frustration. On one hand the guy was admitting he was out of town, he couldn't have met my father, but to save his skin he had to say he had fulfilled his duty. Something shady was going on; his story just didn't jive. When the double-dealer was dismissed from the witness stand, I knew that not nailing him would come back to bite me.

It was my turn on the stand, the moment I'd been waiting for. At last I could tell my story of injustice, and the duplicity of it all, but it was nothing like I'd imagined. While it started out well, when it came time for cross-examination, I was only permitted to respond yes or no to questions carefully crafted to make me look like a heartless wench of a daughter. S. also had a little surprise tucked neatly in his sleeve. After my father died, this snake, painstakingly searched through all of my dad's correspondence, confiscating every letter and card I'd ever sent him. He pored over every word, artfully highlighting in golden yellow any line, word, or sentence that could be misconstrued or taken out of context. Out of a tender two-page letter, he'd emphasize fragments such as, "I'm sorry you're upset that I moved to New York." Then he insisted I read only the highlighted lines aloud. I refused to be railroaded. Despite his boisterous objections, I defused his ambush by continuing to read my words in their entirety. When that ambush didn't work, he tried to further discredit me by blurting, "Your honor, I don't think her parents were even married."

It seemed this creep had a personal vendetta against me. Even if my parents hadn't been married, did that mean he should inherit my family's estate? Not if I could help it.

S.'s wife was next on the hot seat. She actually admitted barely knowing my father. When asked how she felt about his sexual transformation she replied, "It was an abomination against God."

I wondered if she realized what she was saying, the importance of her testimony. Why would my father bequeath almost a million dollars to someone he hardly knew and who deemed him an abomination?

My two radiant allies, Patti, the quintessential actress, and Miss Pamela, a bestselling authoress, were quite the engaging witnesses. They recounted numerous droll occasions with my dad and testified to his constant near-comatose state and his extraordinary appearance after the sex change. They each recalled my father never missing an opportunity to tearfully lament how I was all he had left in the world, and how when he died I'd be a well-to-do woman.

I was proud of myself. I'd put up the good fight, but the question of the independent review plagued me. Would my case hang on the letter of the law, or would the judge see the real picture? After the trial there was nothing left to do but wait for the court's decision.

I spent the next arduous week going over every detail of the trial in my head. I prayed to God, Jesus, Allah, any saint that would listen. I promised, "Dear Lord, if you just let me prevail, I'll use the money to go to college, and I'll get a degree in psychology." I'd be a comfort like Dr. Deshler, the man who had helped me out of my food-poisoning pickle.

Five days later I got the call. The judge had ruled in my favor. S. and his wife were ordered to immediately return all properties and cash to me, and the twenty thousand dollars gift to the mother-in-law was rescinded. I could hardly believe my ears! I had won!

Of course, it wouldn't be that simple. Mr. S. refused to comply with the order. And he still refused to hand over the accounting of the cash.

A month later we were all back at the courthouse, baking in Palm Springs, awaiting an order from the honorable judge. The good judge ordered sanctions against S. of $250 for each day he withheld my property, but even that didn't do the trick. My own lawyer wasn't very reassuring, either. He just shook his head, saying, "I don't know, I've never experienced anything like this."

Of course not. This was me; nothing was ever simple in my life. With the sanctions amassing into the thousands, S. finally relented. He reluctantly handed over the cash, the Cobra, and some kind of accounting, but this was just the beginning of my woes.

Along with the assets came another bit of news: Mrs. S. was appealing the judgment.

I still wasn't satisfied with the accounting. I sat at my desk for days on end, surrounded by piles of papers and reams of receipts, trying to figure out just where the money had gone. I had copious columns of hand-scrawled addition, subtraction, and multiplication. I was dizzy with numbers swirling in my brain, and my lack of formal education didn't help. I remembered complaining to my seventh-grade math teacher, "Why do I have to know fractions? I'm never gonna need them."

I was in control of the estate, had done my homework, and felt fairly confident I would win the appeal, but then came a new snag.

Supposedly the appellate court ordered arbitration, meaning they wanted me to try and settle out of court. Settle, after all this? No, thank you. I wanted to take my chances at the courthouse, but my lawyer said I didn't have a choice; it was mandated by the appellate court.

To be sure, he put doubt in my step by telling me the appeals court was a fifty-fifty gamble. Most likely I'd win, but it was possible I could lose it all. My brain was beginning to ache. I couldn't think clearly about this anymore. It had consumed two years of my sweet life. I'd become all about a court case, it was my focus, my conversation, it even invaded my dreams like a broken record. I was determined to triumph, but on the other hand, I was almost willing to pay just to make it go away, and to move on with my life. Unknown to me, the purpose of the arbitration was to whittle me down to the marrow.

I arrived in Riverside County at the crack of nine, armed with unruffled conviction and laden with confidence. I imagined it would be like the round table, that we'd sit at the table board and hash it out in a civil manner. Maybe I'd even concede and toss them a small bone just to get it over with. It turned out to be a bit more covert. I'd almost forgotten who I was dealing with, and I fell headfirst into the pit.

After ten onerous hours of strategic double talk, I understood that I was about to give away a third of my inheritance, but not without the understanding that in return I'd get a full accounting. A handwritten document was drawn up stating that I was to receive a full and final accounting, and at that point I *shall* hand over one third of the residue. I read and reread every locution like I was trying to crack a secret code, then I questioned my lawyer like it was the Spanish Inquisition.

"Are you sure this can't be disputed? Are you positive I'm not signing my rights away?"

I sensed my attorney was a breath away from becoming annoyed.

"Yes, it's as I've told you; we'll go after them until they give the accounting."

"But what if they refuse?" I asked.

"You're in possession of the estate," he assured me. "You don't have to pay anything till you're completely satisfied."

He seemed quite certain that the document was to my benefit, and spurred me on to endorse. My inner voice was screaming, *"Don't sign!"*

There stood the arbitrator, Mr. S. and his wife, her attorney, my attorney, the appellate attorney, and my son Damian. Seven tired people stood around waiting for me to come to a decision. It seemed to me that if the opposition was satisfied with the covenant, something was awry. Was I just being overly paranoid? To make the situation all the more pressing, all summer I'd been working on the movie *Town and Country*, standing in and photo doubling for Diane Keaton. My morning call was at 5:00 A.M. If I left right now, by the time I got back to Los Angeles, I might get five hours' sleep. My attorney had a good point. I was in possession of the estate—what was the worst that could happen?

A month had passed, and still no accounting. It was starting to look like my own attorney had sold me down the river. It turned out the agreement I had signed actually was airtight except for two little definitive words: "I shall." In *Black's Law Dictionary* the simple word "shall" is as good as a done deal. Mr. S. got around our accounting agreement by avowing the original ledger was the final and true document. I demanded we go back to court; I would simply deliver a paper trail of documentation to the judge.

To my utter astonishment, the magistrate couldn't have been less interested. He sternly spoke: "Miss James, you have signed an agreement which is to be upheld. Please take under consideration the waste of the court's time and money you are costing all involved."

He refused to even accept my files. I felt like I'd crashed into a cement wall. I quickly hired another attorney, who reviewed the agreement and confirmed, "This is unconscionable! You never should have signed this."

The next step was another five grand to start an additional lawsuit, this one confronting my previous attorney. Did I really want to go through this a second time? I was losing my thirst for justice, or the lack of it. I just wanted to get back to my life, release myself from the legal stratagem and intrigue.

I called my original attorney and asked, "How much is it going to cost to make you all go away?"

I wrote out the checks and Mr. Toad's slippery ride came to a peaceful repose. I felt like I'd gone ten rounds with Muhammad Ali and come out miraculously only slightly bruised. I'd certainly given S. a run for the money and managed to retrieve a portion of my inheritance. There was still a pit in my stomach that felt like a bitter pill. I still felt flagrantly robbed. But like everything else in life, I'd get over it.

So now what? I'd fought the good fight and the movie with Diane Keaton was completed. Oh yes, there was still my deal with the Lord, my vow to use my inheritance to get an education.

I called UCLA and inquired about their psychology program. The counselor said I'd need a copy of my high school transcripts. High school transcripts? I'd barely made it to the seventh grade. In my sporadic adolescence I'd attended eleven different elementary schools and two junior highs. There had been no prom night or high school reunions for me. It appeared I was going to have to start from the beginning. I made an appointment at Hollywood High to take the required GED.

The general knowledge and English exams were a breeze, but when I got to the mathematics, especially algebra, I was lost. I had no concept of equating numerals with the alphabet; it was like trying to decipher hieroglyphics. It also appeared that I was going to need some class credits that would cost at least a year of my cherished time. I was a fifty-year-old girl with little desire to do a term at the local high school. Determined to keep my promise to the Almighty, I leaped the hurdle and enrolled in the regional city college. Thankfully no one checked up or asked me to furnish a high school diploma. I was free and eager to learn. Never mind that I was the oldest student in the lecture hall: I'd made it to college.

My initial course was chemistry of the brain. I'd always believed I was somewhat cerebral, but compared to the immensity of knowledge and wisdom obtainable at the college, I knew naught. I felt like applauding after each and every inspiring lecture. I was learning the science of synapses, serotonin uptake, and the chemistry of gray matter. I could almost feel my dendrites branching, reaching to make a connection. Besides the psychology there were the prerequisite classes. I opted for history of film, anatomy, and the mandatory English 101.

I'd read some of the classics, loved the Irish poets, and thought Shakespeare was a prophet, but creative writing was not one of my innate abilities. It took me an hour just to compose a Post-it note. I was sure English class would be a bore, but I lucked out and got an illuminating professor abounding with whimsical tales. Mr. Dumonte was a romantic Italian American who spent the first hour of his classes speaking of his pilgrimages to the old country. He'd tell us dreamy, vivid stories of the Spanish Steps and the Bridge of Sighs, then take us on a journey through the Italian countryside and farmlands.

"Now it's your turn," he'd say. "Tell me a story, write me something you're passionate about."

For fear of my mother's wrath and obsession with perfection, I'd always been self-conscious and afraid not to be perfect. I had a creative soul, but I always got lost in the detail. Mr. Dumonte made it so easy: "Just write what's in your heart."

In the midst of my spirited enlightenment, I had a somber

epiphany. Even if I spent the next two decades buried in books, I was running out of time. I may not have looked or felt like it, but I was now fifty-two years old, over half a century. I wished I had had this opportunity forty years earlier. In the words of Terry Malloy, I realized I could have been a contender. I had been too busy focusing most of my life on survival, raising a child and trying to decode the mysterious opposite sex. I hadn't a clue there was so much more. I always felt like I'd fallen to earth via the heavens, and begun my journey without even so much as a reference manual. On the plus side, God gave me a pretty face, an inquisitive intellect, and Mimi, my guiding light, to help soften the fall.

19

*D*uring my second semester of edification, my mystical grandmother began to ail. Mimi had been on the planet a hundred years, and for the first time was showing signs of wear. It was only two months ago we were energetically trawling the thrift shops for lost treasures before trotting off to Dupar's for a bite of custard pie. She still delighted in dragging out her beaded silk finery from the forties, and we'd play dress-up like a pair of schoolgirls.

One morning Mimi called asking, "Could you come over, love? I'm not feeling so well." After one look at my beloved Mimi, I called the paramedics, who swooped her up in an ambulance and sped her off to Cedars-Sinai hospital. The doctors did a barrage of blood tests, and her physician informed me, "I'm sorry to have to tell you this, but your mother has cancer."

"She's my grandmother," I said.

Not only was she my grandmother, she was my son's great-grandmother and a great-great-grandmother to boot. We were five generations alive.

Mimi was so amazingly well preserved that the doctors decided to go ahead and operate on my hundred-year-old girl. She got through the surgery without a hitch, but the trauma left her as weak as a babe. Her physician assured me that with a bit of rest she'd be good to go. The bad news was that, against her bitter protest, she was being admitted to a nursing home until she was strong enough to walk on her own.

The atmosphere at the convalescent home was about as joyful as during the plague. The dreary green hallways were lined in wheelchairs with worn, tired souls either slumped comatose or mumbling to the cosmos. All these little spirits with their inner light barely a glint. I padded past the nurses' station through a maze of lifeless corridors and eerie groans until I found my sweet Mimi.

"There you are . . . ," I said cheerfully, as if it wasn't so bad here.

Before I could even get through the door Mimi cried, "Thank God you're here, my prayers have been answered. Catherine, if you have even a shred of love for me, please take me out of here!"

"Mimi, it's just for a few days."

But she wouldn't be calmed. "Catherine, please," she begged. "Don't leave me here. I'll die."

I could feel my heart shattering. I remembered all the times she had come to my rescue, how she had sat up all night holding my hand when I had scarlet fever, the way she fought so hard for me in the courts. My soft-spoken angel woman had never once let me down. I wondered, was it illegal? Would I be able to get her past the nurses station? What about her IV, and oxygen? I envisioned myself maneuvering her body into my car. "All right," I said to myself, "I think I can do this."

"Mimi, if you can sit up on your own, I'll take you home."

"I can," she said.

She grabbed onto the bed rail, struggled to rise, then fell back to the pillow.

"No, I can't," she moaned.

I felt like Judas but realized there was no way I could even get her out of the bed by myself, much less up the stairs to her home. It seemed like I was helpless to do anything but try to comfort her. I had the nurse bring her a sedative, and I held her hand till she fell off to sleep.

As the days passed Mimi became as fragile as a petal, and her chances of going home looked slim to nil.

During her infirmity I still had two final exams at the college. I was propped up on the sofa trying to finish the last dry chapter of biological psychology when I felt an unsettling jolt. I knew instantly it was my grandmother; she was about to die. I grabbed my coat and sped down San Vicente Boulevard, praying to make it there in time. At 10:30 the halls were ghostly still, not even a shadow of a night nurse to be found. When I got to my grandmother's room, I whispered, "I'm here, Mimi."

With her eyes still closed, in a soft weary voice she said, "That's good, love."

Her breathing was short and steady, almost like someone in childbirth, like she was propelling herself somewhere big. My eyes instantly flooded with tears. I held onto her soft familiar hand and asked, "Is it peaceful, Mimi, or are you afraid?"

"It's both," she said.

I turned off the light over her bed, leaving a small ray of light illuminating the room from the hall.

"Is there anything you want?" I whispered. "Can I do anything for you?"

With her eyes still closed she asked, "I'd like a little water, please."

I gently held her sweet head and gave her a last sip.

"Mimi, I want you to know that every loving compassionate trait I possess, my awareness of beauty and grace, my artistic nature, every good thing about me is you, a gift from you."

For a brief moment she opened her eyes and replied, "It was all worth it, then."

Those were her last words to me: "It was all worth it."

I wanted to keep talking with her. I wanted to know where she was going, what it was like, but this was her moment.

It was time to let my Mimi be. I thought how perfect that it was just the two of us, just like when I was little. I ran my hands from the top of her head to the soles of her feet.

"I've loved you so much, Mimi. You were everything to me."

I put my head down, and asked the angels to come and take her softly. And they did.

All the beautiful women in my family had one thing in common: They all suffered from vanity. Mimi was not an exception. For years, even before she became ill, she always asked me to promise that when she died I would be the one to do her makeup for her funeral. After one hundred years she still took pride in her carefully arched eyebrows and lily white complexion. The day before her burial I packed a sachet of cosmetics and headed for the mortuary to keep our pact. It never occurred to me that there might be a problem getting in. I marched into the parlor and said, "I'm here to see my grandmother."

The undertaker said it was impossible, that I'd have to wait till the service in the morning.

"But I can't wait; I have to see her now."

He said he was sorry but it was against policy, and I'd have to come back tomorrow.

"But she's here. Why can't I see her?"

When I explained I wasn't leaving without seeing her, the man went into another area, and I could hear him whispering with the staff. The next thing I knew a room was prepared for me to visit.

I was taken to a pure white compartment, and there she lay. Mimi was tightly swathed in white muslin and her shoulder-length straight hair was freshly combed back away from her face. There were small windows that were too high to see out of, but shafts of natural light illuminated the room through the panes, and Mimi looked like some kind of angel. I remembered looking at her two nights earlier, when she was actually leaving her body. As she was dying her face visibly changed. The few lines and wrinkles she possessed had melted before my eyes, and her skin became smooth and taut. In this spotless white room Mimi looked as pure as snow; it felt sacrilegious to start putting paint on her face. I decided that just a brush of pale fingernail polish, and she'd be good to go. I tugged on the muslin where her hands were bound inside, but she was wrapped so tightly, it wouldn't budge. I'd have to unwrap half her body to reach her fingertips, but then how was I going to get the cloth back tight the way it was? I thought, what if the funeral director comes in and finds me and Mimi in a heap of unraveled cotton; he'd think I was a nut! No, she was perfect just the way she was. I spoke out loud to my grandmother, "You don't need any makeup today, Mimi. You already look beautiful."

There was nothing left to do but stand by her still body. I wanted to inhale and hold on to our last moment. My little tears turned into big sobs. I became so overcome I had to turn away from her and knelt to the floor weeping, with my hands hiding my face. In the midst of my emotional cloudburst of tears I somehow floated up into another perspective. I saw the two of us from above, like looking down at a tragic Renaissance painting. Mimi laid out in white, and me to the side with my head in my hands, grief-stricken. I had a clear feeling that we had experienced this before, and that this would not be the last time.

Except for Diana, my whole family was gone. My father, grandparents, aunts, even my young cousin had departed early. I never really knew Lois, but I'd heard she died at just fifty-nine.

While sorting through Mimi's belongings I discovered a chest of drawers packed tight with notebooks, loose binders, and a cachet of sealed manila envelopes. I suppose for copyright reasons, Mimi had mailed the unopened envelopes to herself. I thought I knew everything about Mimi, but discovered that her secret desire was to be a writer. The bureau contained original screenplays, short stories, and unfinished compositions, some postdated as far back as the forties. I also came across a stunning little gem addressed to my grandson. John is fourteen now, so she must have written it when he was born. After the funeral I said to John, "I have a letter to you from your great-great-grandmother. Would you like to have it?"

John thought about it, then sweetly replied, "No, not yet, Grand-mother Catherine."

20

*I*t had been almost two years since Mimi had left the earth, and at last my life seemed to be settling down. Then out of the blue I got a call from my half brother Etienne. He called to say that our mother was in the hospital and nearing death. Wow, my mighty mother was dying! I'm not sure why, but I instinctively felt an urge to see her while I still had the opportunity.

Nevada City is one of the more beautiful places on the planet, and the place where my mother was living. It's a beautiful old gold rush town founded in 1849. It's an hour from Lake Tahoe, and is surrounded by lakes, rivers, and tall, green pines. The city's historic architecture is still stunningly intact, and even has gaslit streets. I checked into the Victorian Holbroke hotel, the same place where Mark Twain had once lodged, and prepared to revisit my daunting past.

Tien, as he likes to be called, still lived in the area, and met me at one of the quaint old dining halls on Main Street. He brought along a bottle of cabernet, and we chattered and laughed all through our tasty salmon pasta. I learned that my younger brother loves camping, he likes fishing and snowboards at midnight, the same things I like. He's a hopeful romantic just like me, and I instantly adored him. Tien was the lucky one. He came at the tail and less damaging end of Diana's reign. He also had little knowledge of our frightful relationship. I was having such a nice time with him that I'd almost forgotten why I'd come here. When Tien asked if I was ready to go visit our mother, I felt a stiff snap back to reality. Now that I was actually here, I wasn't so sure. I felt almost dizzy with fear of the unknown. I'd just driven seven hours to get here, and now I wanted to go home. Tien reassurd me that if Diana became too unpleasant, we didn't have to stay. I gulped down my last bit of wine, and off we drove to the Maiden View Manor.

The winding country roads were as dark as pitch, and on our way to the nursing home a heavy snow began to fall. It was just us, me and my brother, speeding through the night, a little spot on the universe with angel ice falling around us. At that moment I realized there was nothing to be afraid of. Everything was in its perfect place.

In my mind and memory I'd been expecting an encounter with the dark queen. Instead I found a skeletal, tiny little woman with an oxygen tube strapped to her face. I barely recognized her. I'd never seen my mother without her heavy Egyptian eyeliner, and her arms and legs were reduced to paper-thin skin clinging to protruding, fragile bones. Diana was only seventy-three and now weighed less than her age. It took her a moment to realize who I was. Then she coolly looked away, saying, "Catherine, I wasn't expecting you." Then she proceeded to ignore my existence.

I dismissed her snub with a smile, and cheerfully beamed, "Well here I am."

I wasn't really sure why I was there. There was no lost love between us, but she was the only mother I would ever have. In a perfect world I would have been here for my mother when she was dying. I always wanted to be the devoted daughter, and now I had a captive audience.

The ice broke when I set Jack, my playful three-pound Yorkshire terrier, loose on her hospital bed. It's not easy being aloof with a bounding puppy attacking and licking your face. When Tien stepped out of her room for a breath of fresh air, my mother spoke, "Isn't Tien just a wonderful boy?"

I agreed that she was lucky to have him. Then she made a chilling statement, something that only I could comprehend. "He's the only one the witches didn't get to."

Her words practically knocked me over. Did I hear her right? I instantly envisioned a pair of charred black hags with long curved fingernails reaching out toward me. Then, in a whoosh they disappeared back into the top of my mother's head.

I knew precisely what she was saying, but I had to ask, "What do you mean by that?"

She looked clear into my eyes. Her stare was so deep that I felt it in my heart. I wanted to look away, but I held her gaze.

"You know exactly what I mean."

In a split second my childhood played back like a video on rewind. I saw myself locked in the closet and bound to a chair in the dark. I felt her rage, what it was like hiding in bushes for safety, and being abandoned to strangers. Maybe it was the witches.

My mother couldn't have been more eloquent. It was a stunning admission, and maybe her way of apologizing, at the same time relinquishing all responsibility of her prior unconscionable wickedness. Of course it wasn't her. It was the witches. In a strange way her words were comforting. *She knew.* I suddenly realized why I was here. I'd come to forgive her.

With that bit of powerful wisdom stored safely in my soul, I wanted to do something nice for her.

"Mother, would you like me to do your makeup for you?" Without hesitation she answered, "Yes."

She still used the cake eyeliner with a sable brush, of which she owned several. As I dug though her deep makeup case looking for the right pot of black, she snapped, "Be careful to put everything back in its right place. No, Catherine, that doesn't belong there."

Diana didn't disappoint; even on her deathbed she was still domineering, and salty as brine.

"Yes, mother."

It had been a long time since I'd heard the words "Yes, mother" come from my lips. The interesting thing was that instead of being scary, now the words sounded almost comical. I carefully lined her green eyes in matte black. Not the way I would have done it, but heavier, the way she liked it. With some Joan Crawford eyebrows, and a wisp of rouge she was quite pleased with herself.

It was after midnight, and time to be getting back to the hotel. I kissed her cheek and promised to be back soon. I was surprised when she asked, "When, when are you coming back?"

"I'm not sure, but soon."

Tien and I were halfway out the door, but something was still missing. I walked back to her bed and touched her bone-thin leg. "I love you, mother."

But did I really love her? My words felt detached and forced. What I really meant was, I wish I could have loved you. That was the truth, but maybe this was a start.

I would have stayed on in Nevada City a bit longer, but I was still working for John Paul DeJoria. He'd recently sold the Hilltop hideaway in Beverly Hills, and I was now managing and living on his fourteen-acre fortress in Malibu. John Paul had said to take as much time as I needed, but someone had to be there to look after the estate.

I kept in daily contact with Tien and urged my reluctant brother

Scot to go back up with me and at least pay a last visit. I did my best to locate Elizabeth, but she could not be found. We were an estranged family of four with little in common except that we all belonged to the same unique club. In succession we'd all experienced the ominous wrath of the witches. We belonged to a mother who could not love, and tried her best to break each of us.

I got the fateful call from Tien when it was time. My brother Scot was pretty much resolved to stay away, but then agreed to go if I drove and it didn't cost him out of pocket.

Tien had taken Diana out of the Maiden View home and had brought her home to die in her own Victorian bed. When we arrived our mother appeared so shocking that Scot had trouble looking. He thought she was already dead. The once beautiful Diana had degenerated so badly that she looked like a picked-over carcass. Her thighs were thinner than my wrists, but she still managed to hoist herself in and out of bed. The odd thing was that she still had a full head of natural auburn hair. I felt a fright. Was this what was going to happen to me, too? Then I remembered how pretty and peaceful Mimi had looked when she died. Hopefully I'd end up somewhere in the middle.

My two brothers were sharing a bottle of wine in the other room, and I was alone with my mother. I sat on the edge of her bed, trying to figure out what I was feeling. The answer was, not much. It was nothing like when Mimi died. I couldn't have mustered up a tear for my mother if my life depended on it. Why was I really here again? I brought along the vanilla ice cream she'd asked for, and was hand-feeding her tiny spoonfuls, when out of the blue, she said, "I'm sorry for hurting you, Catherine." Those were the magic words, and from my eyes tears began to drop like salted rain. "Why are you crying?" she asked.

"Because I really wanted to love you; we could have been friends." For the first time in my life she softly stroked my hair like a mother would, and it broke my unsuspecting heart. I wanted to say, "Snap out of it, wake up, please don't die yet!" I wanted more time with her, but now it was too late.

My mother's soft touch confused me. Our relationship had been a fine dance between fear and self-preservation. If she had not been melting, would we have had this moment? Her touch felt like sparkling electric shocks with immaculate healing. It wasn't me as the grown woman. In my mind's eye I saw the child. It was like being bathed in the sweetest water, and the warmest light. There was a divine mutual forgiveness, and the past no longer mattered.

Epilogue

Bob Dylan had been right about my mother. She did indeed
end up all alone. There was no funeral or fanfare, not even
a memorial. There was only a quiet cremation, and my half
brother Tien is the keeper of her ashes.

The whole extraordinary cast responsible for my being alive has
now perished. Sometimes I drive past the big house on Ozeta Terrace.
It's still rich with mysterious memories, and I think to myself, "Where
is everyone? You've all left without me."

In reality, except for Mimi, I never felt a deep connection to anyone
in my crazy family. I desperately wanted to feel close, but it was like
watching impenetrable actors in a very strange play. In an interesting
way they inadvertently gave me extraordinary gifts. My mother's cal-
lousness gave me a deep sense of compassion and the will of an army.
The lack of stability and permanence gave me freedom to do whatever
I could imagine.

When my son was born it somehow broke a volatile mold. We remain close as peas in a pod, and have great laughs remembering our never-dull past. I have remained friendly with Patrick and Joseph. Patrick has remarried, and is happily back in his homeland of England. Joseph is still married to the same girl, and interestingly enough they adopted a girl from Vista del Mar, the very same orphanage I ran away from. Denny Laine has also remarried and lives in Las Vegas. He has reconnected with Damian, and we all get along like old friends. I'm grateful to Denny, as he was the one who opened the door to remarkable places and unheralded times. He also gave me my best treasure, a son. Damian is happily married to a Buddhist beauty, and I have a teenage grandson, John, who tells me he loves me the best. I have created my own happy family, the one I always dreamed of.

Index